Anglo-Catholic Worship:
An Evangelical Appreciation after 150 years

Edited by
Colin Buchanan
*Principal of St. John's College, Bramcote, Nottingham
Member of the Church of England Liturgical Commission*

GROVE BOOKS

BRAMCOTE   NOTTS.   NG9 3DS

CONTENTS

		Page
	Introduction: by Colin Buchanan	3
1.	'These holy mysteries': by John Fenwick	9
2.	'This child is regenerate': by Colin Buchanan	17
3.	'Seven times daily will I praise you': by David Cutts	23
4.	'Magnify your office': by Michael Sansom	27
5.	'Whose sins you forgive they are forgiven': by David Gregg	32
6.	'The beauty of holiness': by David Parkes	35
7.	'Every knee shall bow': by Charles Hutchins	41
8.	'Holy chant and psalm': by Robin Leaver	45
9.	'Many happy returns': by Colin Buchanan	49

Copyright the respective authors 1983

THE CHAPTER TITLES

are derived as follows: chapter 1, from the BCP communion service; chapter 2, from the BCP infant baptism rite; chapter 3, from Tract 75 (quoting Psalm 119.164); chapter 4, from Tract 1 (alluding to Rom. 11.13); chapter 5 from the BCP ordinal (drawing upon John 20.23); chapter 6, from J. S. B. Monsell's hymn (drawing upon Psalm 96.9); chapter 7, from Phil 2.10; chapter 8, from G. Rorison's hymn *Three in One and One in Three*; chapter 9, from English social idiom.

THE CONTRIBUTORS

John Fenwick is chaplain of Trinity College, Bristol
David Cutts is domestic chaplain to the Bishop of St. Edmundsbury and Ipswich
Michael Sansom is vice-principal of Ridley Hall, Cambridge
David Gregg is principal of Romsey House, Cambridge
David Parkes is vicar of Bear Park, Durham
Charles Hutchins is principal of the Church Army Wilson Carlisle Training College, Blackheath
Robin Leaver is librarian of Latimer House, Oxford, and priest-in-charge of Cogges, Witney, Oxon.

ACKNOWLEDGMENTS

All the contributors acknowledge the help they have received from the Group for the Renewal of Worship, and also in several cases from anglo-catholic friends. However, each author is responsible for his own contribution, and no attempt has been made to produce a total identity of outlook. The cover picture is by Peter Ashton

C.O.B.

First Impression March 1983
ISSN 0306–0608
ISBN 0 907536 44 1

INTRODUCTION
by Colin Buchanan

'The following Sunday, July 14th [1833], Mr. Keble preached the Assize Sermon in the University pulpit. It was published under the title of "National Apostasy". I have ever considered and kept the day, as the start of the religious movement of 1833.'[1]

'The religious movement of 1833'—the phrase stirs the emotions still. 150 years on, it is clear that the movement has had a revolutionary effect on the Church of England, and indeed on the Anglican Communion at large. The doctrines of apostolic succession, eucharistic sacrifice, baptismal regeneration, sacramental confession, petitions for the departed, and a host of others, virtually unknown before the nineteenth century in Anglicanism, have not only flourished and grown, but have also frequently been treated as foundational to the whole sense of *being* Anglican. Ideas let loose in the nineteenth century flourished and grew as they seized men's minds. Opponents went to law to stop ideas, and the ideas banked up behind the legal dams till their force broke the barriers and swept on with greater force. Anglo-catholicism has rewritten Anglican church history, reshaped the face of Anglican parish life, and done something less tangible but equally important to the very soul of Anglicanism. It has inspired its followers, infuriated its opponents, and, we have no doubt, delighted and frustrated the angels in equal degrees. We who live late on in the twentieth century, if we would believe in God at all in England today, inevitably have our thinking touched and shaped by this astonishing force within the Church of England.

But the authors here are not anglo-catholics. Indeed, we descend, in a manner of speaking, from the most fervent opponents of the movement. We are fully capable of opposing it still. As I write, I am myself engaged in a synodical battle about priestly absolution which exhibits all the classic symptoms of nineteenth century clashes.[2] And yet this Study is conceived in a less-than-adversarial way. In part, we have to acknowledge that there never were simply two clashing forces in the Church of England—us (the 'goodies'—evangelical), and them (the 'baddies'—anglo-catholic). The matter has been more complex than that, and an earlier third force—Liberalism—has often united evangelicals and anglo-catholics in defending the same ground, whilst a latter-day one—the Charismatic Movement—has often united them in sharing the same experience. Furthermore, a true confrontational encounter of Christians does not leave both sides just as they were before. *That* can only be secured by ensuring there is no real encounter. When encounter does take place, misconceptions are cleared away, ground between is narrowed, emphases of the other side are taken aboard, and a quest for truly 'catholic' Christianity is initiated. That sort of dynamic helps distinguish Christians from politicians.

[1] J. H. Newman *Apologia Pro Vita Sun,* the concluding sentences of Part III. Others of course would date the 'movement' from the meeting at H. J. Rose's Rectory at Hadleigh in Suffolk on 25 July 1833. And a case can also be made for dating the Tractarian Movement from the first three Tracts—9 September 1833.

[2] This battle ended in February 1983 with a result charted in chapter 5, pp.34 below.

ANGLO-CATHOLIC WORSHIP: AN EVANGELICAL APPRECIATION AFTER 150 YEARS

However, lest we come too quickly to the charitable features of the encounter, I set the scene with two gloriously polarized presentations of the matter. One is from the anglo-catholic Frank Weston, Bishop of Zanzibar from 1908 to 1924. In one of his early letters home he wrote:

> 'Out here we get heartily sick of the present confusion of faith at home . . . the Faith and the CMS religion are expressed in such clean-cut lines out in the Mission Field that it requires all one's past experience . . . to keep from cutting oneself adrift from English thought in religion. We go our own way: find it to be the only way: and we cannot conceive of any other way . . .'[1]

Since I first read it, I have greatly treasured (as a collector's piece) the swaggering confidence of that 'The Faith' and 'The CMS religion'. My other witness is Stephen Neill. In replying to Kirk's great but unsuccessful attempt to say the final word on apostolic succession, *The Apostolic Ministry* (1946), Stephen Neill wrote:

> 'We must not deceive ourselves by refusing to face the fact tht what makes one give different answers from another is that we do not believe in the same kind of God, or at least do not believe in God in the same way . . . Those of us who reject the doctrine of Church and ministry set forth in *The Apostolic Ministry* reject it, not on grounds of minute differences on points of archaeological interpretation, but because we cannot recognize as Christian the doctrine of God, which seems to underlie this imposing theological edifice.'[2]

If the present authors move on to somewhat happier conclusions than these two particular instances would suggest, yet it with a real sense in their hearts that they have at least *felt* the polarization to which these citations bear testimony, and in each case they would have been found on the evangelical side of such a divide.

We are not here presenting history, or at least not in a chronologically unfolding style. The Study is too short, the ground is already well-trodden, and our birthday present to the heirs of the Oxford Movement cries out less for data than for value-judgments. It is our attempt to *reflect* on what we know, and we hope that such reflection will prove a true mirror to those for whom we write it. We beg their pardon now if our mirror distorts the truth. We can only write what we have seen.

Nor do we view this as a whole survey of anglo-catholicism. We are not here concerned to chart any features other than anglo-catholic *worship*. The yearnings towards Rome, the creation of theological Colleges, the vaunting of celibacy, the founding of religious communities, the distinguished line of academics, these and a host of other matters are outside our purview. They may well hang together with a whole religious 'world-view' which is dubbed anglo-catholicism,

---

[1] H. Maynard Smith *Frank Bishop of Zanzibar* (S.P.C.K., London, 1926) pp.154-5.
[2] S. C. Neill (ed.) *The Ministry of the Church: A Review by Various authors of a book entitled The Apostolic Ministry* (Canterbury Press, London and Edinburgh, 1947) p.28.

INTRODUCTION

and, if so, they belong to the movements we observe in worship. But, for the sake of a short Study, we have tried to concentrate our gaze on those parts of Christian worship—i.e. the visible and external parts—which a man may actually *see* and *evaluate*.

Nor, even then, is our conspectus exhaustive. We have not touched on anglo-catholic preaching, though the words of Michael Marshall, Bishop of Woolwich, still ring in my ears: 'From one point of view, the Oxford Movement could be viewed as the rise of a company of mission-preachers.' We have not touched on the invocation of saints, though it could yet prove one of the most obstinate barriers between Roman Catholicism and biblical/evangelical Christianity—and it has an open history in anglo-catholicism. We have only skirted round petitions for the departed, though they have been a thoroughly controversial matter in print, and in Synod, and at actual funerals, for over a hundred years. We have passed by the resurgence of shrines and pilgrimages and the cult of holy places. And we have said little about the role of the bishop in worship, although we have experienced an astonishing liturgical 'cult of the personality' (and cult of the mitre) stemming from the other doctrines and policies which are examined here.

That said, we return to our theme. Worship is at the heart of the 'catholic' revival. Worship has been the storm-centre of so many controversies. Worship is, in any case, the great interest which binds the present team of evangelicals together. And so anglo-catholic worship is our theme. And it may help if we give here the barest outlines of the eras of the history of that worship which we discern, an outline which all the authors take for granted in what they write.

Firstly, there is the period of the Tracts. This was the period which Newman calls one of 'proving' the 'cannon'[1]—i.e. would the framework of the Church of England prove capable of sustaining the much more powerful charge which the Tractarians were introducing?[2] It was conducted largely at the level of *ideas*. Parish worship did not look much altered, though some of the leaders were using the Roman breviary for their own devotions, and Pusey at least was hearing confessions from the late 1830s onwards.[3] The tone of the Tracts was to preach up the Prayer Book—in particular searching out features long lapsed, such as the observance of fasts and vigils and eves—and to emphasize its continuity with the Catholic past. In spirit the reformers had no doubt gone too far—but in letter they had bequeathed a fully 'catholic' inheritance to the Church of England, and all it needed was drawing out and enforcing. Would the 'cannon' bear this load? To Newman the cannon split when it was fired, but to many others it did sustain it, albeit with much recoil and disruption.

---

[1] Newman *Letters* II, 318, quoted by E. A. Know *The Tractarian Movement* (Putnam, London and New York, 1933) p.247.

[2] Knox *op. cit.* entitles his chapter about Tract 90 as 'Proving the Cannon'.

[3] 'It is now [1850] some twelve years I suppose since I was first called upon to exercise this office.' (H. P. Liddon *Life of E. B. Pusey D.D.*(Longmans, London, 1898) Vol. iii, p.269).

ANGLO-CATHOLIC WORSHIP: AN EVANGELICAL APPRECIATION AFTER 150 YEARS

From 1850 to 1904 the 'catholicizing' of the parishes spread and spread. Colour and movement and Roman Catholic ceremonial and ornamentation of all sorts was introduced. Romanticism ruled the day. Colour was needed in the drab lives of London's East end. The possibility of martyrdom gave a spice of extra conviction. Celibacy lent its air of mystique and other-worldliness.[1] Rubrics and laws and episcopal utterances were breached freely as the provisions of the Prayer Book were found to be inadequate. And in the latter years, latin usages and permanent reservation (and adoration) of the sacramental elements was added to the innovations which had been paraded before the courts in the famous cases of the years from 1857 to 1872—but had never included such enormities as these! The Royal Commission on Ecclesiastical Discipline (1904-6) was the outcome of it all.

After 1906, all sorts of trends arose. There was a move (following the reports of the Royal Commission, towards textual revision of the liturgy. This lurched its way through Convocations and (from 1920) the National Assembly and, finally, Parliament, and was defeated in Parliament in 1927 and 1928 largely because it permitted reservation—though also because the alternative eucharistic rite provided contained little to attract anglo-catholics in its final form. There was also a touch of triumphalism in the rise of the Anglo-Catholic Congresses from 1920 to 1933—and in these circles the doctrine which prevailed was that, as Catholic priests, the clergy of the Church of England had the 'right' to use Roman rites, to reserve the elements without reference to anybody, and generally to follow their own policies, without respect to Parliament, episcopacy, National Assembly, rubrics or canons, or whatever—so long as it could be dubbed 'Catholic'. The mood of the Congresses was to defy all authorities with that touch of assurance which expected to win. The defiance was improved by the importation of impeccable anglo-catholics from Zanzibar, Korea, and other such places, where full-blown 'catholicism' was not a rebellion but rather by now the established rule.

But a wholly different feature of catholicism was the gentle capture of over half the parishes, and certainly half the episcopate, for a mild, and generally law-abiding, catholicism. Two candles, wafers, the eastward position, fasting before communion, and the debarring of nonconformists without confirmation from communion, became not a 'party' manifestation, but instead within an incredibly short time became thought to be 'normal' Anglicanism.[2] It was this sort of catholicized

---

[1] When the high (but not extreme) churchman Cosmo Gordon Lang went to Portsea in 1896 a letter in the local newspaper alleged that he 'was not ashamed to practise celibacy openly in the street'—but that was because he wore his cassock outdoors! (J. G. Lockhart *Cosmo Gordon Lang* (Hodder and Stoughton, London, 1949) p.121).

[2] The first bishop of the Church of England since the Reformation to wear a mitre was (probably) Edward King (Lincoln 1885-1910). The first Archbishop of Canterbury was Lang in 1929! The last Archbishop of Canterbury to prefer North Side for presiding at communion was Freddie Temple (died 1902). The vesting of ordinands in stoles at ordinations does not seem to have started till the 1920s. And hundreds, if not thousands, of parishes, went over to candles and wafers and eastward position between 1900 and 1940.

INTRODUCTION

'centre' which wanted the 1928 Prayer Book, and this sort which cross-fertilized with modernist thought to produce 'liberal catholicism'.

These divergences between anglo-catholics are exactly what one would expect as numbers increased. The Church of England began to fall neatly into their laps but they were now not agreed among themselves as to the programme to fulfil, nor was vocal opposition lacking in any case. And, in the late twenties and early thirties, a new force was at work. Both pastoral needs in England, and some acquaintance, especially by Gabriel Hebert, with the Roman Catholic continental Liturgical Movement, led to some new moves, most obviously expressed in the rise of the parish communion. This was a distinctly 'catholic' movement, but a highly reforming one. It started a change in parishes which in the post-World War II years was to spread and in its turn capture almost the whole Church of England. Changes in Rome after Vatican II affected it all deeply also, and those who had always looked to Rome for the unchanging and eternal authoritative revelation of how things should be done found themselves with both better models on the one hand, but a more shakeable authority on the other![1]

The later stages have been the years of liturgical revision. Catholics have been far more interested in liturgy than evangelicals, and in the period from 1955 to 1965 Edward Ratcliff and Arthur Couratin and Kenneth Ross and Geoffrey Willis, let alone the ghost of Gregory Dix, ruled supreme on the Liturgical Commission. The great cry in the country was that all revision of the eucharist in the Anglican Communion was in one direction, and the Church of England should catch up. For me personally, the years from 1964, when I joined the Commission, to 1980, when the ASB was published and the old Commission disbanded, were rich in learning and in disputing in Christian love. Some of the points raised in the chapters of this book were worked over then, and the story is told in its own right elsewhere.[2] The programme of revision did not go as it might have done if it had been pursued in the 1940s and 1950s, and from 1965 onwards anglo-catholicism ceased to have so markedly a dominant voice on the Commission (and in the Church Assembly and Synod) as it

---

[1] Thus, all good catholics knew until the 1960s that there is really only one Canon of the Mass (which is why it is *called* the 'Canon' or rule). Thus in England we looked for one Canon. After 1967 we knew that good catholics thought *fopur* Canons was the authoritative norm—and in due course Rite A got four. But in the 1970s we had also discovered that good Catholic practice now also included 'Eucharistic Prayers to be used at Masses with Children'—and suddenly a part of the Church of England discovered that this—which would have been pooh-poohed in the 1960s—was exactly what we now need for pastoral reasons. 'Catholicism' since Vatican II has become volatile in a way which has been breath-taking.

[2] I have written the story up in my own *Recent Liturgical Revision in the Church of England* and the various *Supplements* to it (Grove Booklets on Ministry and Worship 14, 14a, 14b, and 14c). Geoffrey Cuming has done a splendid summary in the new final chapter in the second edition of his *A History of Anglican Liturgy* (MacMillan, London, ²1982). And Ronald Jasper is reputed to be working on the period himself.

had had in the previous years. Evangelicals started to emerge from their ghettoes and enter true dialogue, and the results were far from an overriding rampant catholic programme.

Without going further into events on the Liturgical Commission I would like to draw attention to two other features of this new encounter between evangelicals and anglo-catholics. At the Keele Congress in 1967 evangelical Anglicans enunciated a doctrine of involvement:
> 'Polemics at long range have at times in the past led us into negative and impoverishing 'anti'-attitudes (anti-sacramental, anti-intellectual, *etc.*) from which we now desire to shake free. We recognize that in dialogue we may hope to learn truths held by others to which we have hitherto been blind, as well as to impart to others truths held by us and overlooked by them.'[1]

In my own life this came true not only in the extended way of serving on the Liturgical Commission, but also in a concentrated and memorable way when two evangelicals and two anglo-catholics wrote (in three months at the end of 1969) *Growing into Union.*[2] Here was a genuine attempt at reformulation by mutual reformation. Our statements on the sacraments (and especially on eucharistic sacrifice) made a deep impression, and many parts of the book have been points of reference since. I cite these 'comings together' as evidence that today's authors are not functioning in a 'they have a different God from us' framework. We have been learning, as well as having various *ne plus ultras* which we have had to emphasize. We are deeply respectful of the catholic tradition in the Church of England. In the last analysis we know why we are *not* anglo-catholics, and are only too ready (as in this Study) to say so. But criticisms we deliver arise not from a general antipathy or overclouding suspicion, but simply on particular matters and on the theological and pastoral merits of each case. We dare to hope that we will be read as those who are ready for both the pain and the challenge of Anglican comprehensiveness, those who are ready to strike a blow for truth as we see it, and yet those who under God most heartily long for unity and concord with people whom we love dearly.

---

[1] P. A. Crowe (ed.) *Keele '67* (Falcon, London, 1967) para. 84, p.37.
[2] Colin Buchanan, E. L. Mascall, J. I. Packer, and the Bishop of Willesden [i.e. Graham Leonard, now Bishop of London] *Growing into Union: Proposals for forming a United Church in England* (S.P.C.K., London, 1970).

1. 'THESE HOLY MYSTERIES'
by John Fenwick

If worship is at the heart of being an anglo-catholic, then without doubt the eucharist is at the heart of that worship. It is the source of his spirituality and the summit of his service of God. Christian man must be 'eucharistic man'[1] for it is in the eucharistic assembly that he finds his true place, and is most truly himself. Anglo-catholics found the eucharist a neglected ordinance in 1833, almost an optional adjunct to normal Anglican worship; within 150 years the movement had turned the Church of England into a eucharist-centred church and had gone a very long way to transform Anglican thinking on the meaning of the rite.

So much history, scholarship, controversy, and devotion, have been centred on the eucharist in the last century and a half, that it is only possible here to tease out three broad strands where the influence of the Tractarians and their heirs has been particularly marked.

1. Doctrinal Issues

We begin where the Tractarians began—with eucharistic doctrine. Has the movement which has made Anglicanism so sacramentally conscious brought about a similar transformation in the Church of England's eucharistic *doctrine?*

Officially, of course, the answer is 'No'. By the terms of the 1974 Worship and Doctrine Measure (Section 4 (1))

> 'every form of service or amendment thereof approved by the General Synod . . . shall be such as in the opinion of the General Synod is neither contrary to, nor indicative of any departure from, the doctrine of the Church of England in any essential matter.'

The point is made in the Preface of the ASB where the doctrine of the Church of England is defined as being grounded in the Scriptures, those Fathers and Councils that are agreeable to the Scriptures, the Thirty-Nine Articles, the Book of Common Prayer, and the Ordinal. These are the terms in which Rite A, Rite B, and all their eucharistic prayers, are to be interpreted. But having said that, it is impossible to deny that the communion rites in the ASB contain what might be termed new areas of eucharistic consciousness. These new concepts derive from the number of sources—in particular biblical theology, early rites, and an increased social awareness[2]—but the willingness to include them alongside the 1662 emphases must be counted one of the fruits of anglo-catholicism.

Arguably, however, this breadth of eucharistic thought is a fruit that has ripened comparatively recently. In retrospect the impressions left by the second and subsequent generations of anglo-catholicism is not of originality and exploration in eucharistic theology but of a wholesale adoption of Roman concepts and usages. This uncritical acceptance of things Roman, with an inability or reluctance to think issues through *on their own merits,* remains one of the most depressing features of so much anglo-catholicism to this day. There have been of course notable exceptions—a scholar like Frere was advocating an epiclesis half a century before Rome decided her texts were deficient without one!

---

[1] G. Dix *The Shape of the Liturgy* (Dacre/Black, London, 1945) p.xviii.
[2] Not to mention Roman forms new and old!

ANGLO-CATHOLIC WORSHIP: AN EVANGELICAL APPRECIATION AFTER 150 YEARS

There are two doctrinal areas which have both claimed attention and produced division.

. . . (a) Eucharistic Presence

A belief in the 'Real Presence' of Christ in (or more or less in) the bread and wine has traditionally lain at the heart of anglo-catholic understanding of the eucharist. Moreover it is perhaps the most enduring element of the movement's whole eucharistic 'programme'. In the majority of parishes which would claim to stand in the anglo-catholic tradition the high-tide of 'ritualism' has receded a long way but, however hazy the congregation may be, for example, on eucharistic sacrifice, there still persists the belief that 'something happens' to the bread and wine: they *become* the Body and Blood of Christ.

Most anglo-catholics (I suspect) find themselves instinctively agreeing with Michael Ramsey who (speaking on the subject of supplementary consecration) said 'After all, the consecration of bread and wine . . . is one of the most stupendous things that ever happens in the physical world . . .'[1]

The problem of believing that something objective 'happens' to the elements is that it raises the question: What is the status of elements not used for communion at a particular service? The Tractarians and their successors faced the question against the background of contemporary Roman practice, and reservation and adoration of the elements, and Benediction with the Blessed Sacrament made it almost impossible for them to answer it in any other terms. In the years from 1880 to 1960 these practices ran riot—often with an air of defiance of more normal Anglicanism accompanying them. Today advertisements in the *Church Times* reveal that Benediction and Processions of the Reserved Sacrament still take place, but in general it seems that as Sunday eucharistic practice has become healthier, the substitute cultus has declined. It certainly does not occupy the centre of the stage as it did in 1928. It was a cultus which sprang from and attested this objective 'Real Presence'. It provoked hostility and division—and seemed to revel in doing so.

For evangelicals, for traditional Tractarians, and for extreme 'Ritualists', references to the 'Body' and the 'Blood' are primarily about the death of Christ, whether the sacrifice is remembered, appropriated, or re-presented. There is however quite a powerful strand in more recent anglo-catholic writing which sees the transformation of the elements as a pledge and firstfruits of the transformation of the universe, and places the emphasis there rather than on the death of Christ.

> 'In Christ and in the Eucharist, God has re-established that original union [*sc.* between himself and the material], he has restored the sacramental nature of the universe. That union is not yet absolutely and transparently achieved, of course, but the Eucharist affirms that it is, even now, being achieved . . .'[2]

---

[1] General Synod, *Report of Proceedings* (CIO, London, vol. 3, no. 1, Feb. 1972) p.160.
[2] Richard Holloway, *Signs of Glory* (D.L.T., London, 1982) p.47.

This incarnational dimension of the eucharist is allied to the desire to make the eucharist the focus and expression of the whole of human activity and aspiration. The idea is persuasive, but how valid a concept is it in the proclaiming of the Lord's death until he comes?

. . . (b) Eucharistic Sacrifice

In what sense is the eucharist a sacrifice? What relationship does the rite performed with bread and wine bear to the sacrifice of Christ on Calvary? The questions were major ones at the Reformation and have never been satisfactorily resolved since. The issue is so immense and multi-faceted that no attempt can be made to summarize it here: I offer instead merely a few impressions.

The first is that many anglo-catholics are not sure *precisely* what they want to say when they assert that the eucharist is a sacrifice. The crude certainties of the last century are no longer acceptable. The second (1868) edition of *The Ritual Reason Why* discussing the meaning of the word 'mass' could say

'The best interpretation derives it from the Hebrew word MISSAH a sacrificial offering . . .'[1]

and could describe the Prayer of Humble Access as

'a humble acknowledgement of (the priest's) own unworthiness to execute the ministry which he is about to perform and of that of the communicants to join with him in the Sacrifice by feasting on the Sacred Victim who is now about to be offered.'[2]

Such starkness would, I think, cause embarrassment to many modern anglo-catholics. A second impression is that evangelicals tend to assume that something similar to this is what anglo-catholics *still* want to say, *because they do not hear any clear alternative*. And yet there are signs that some anglo-catholics honestly want to cut through the entangled polemic and seek the heart of what it is they are asserting. The very fact that Rowan Williams could subtitle his Liturgical Study on eucharistic sacrifice, *'The Roots of a Metaphor'*[3] raises new hopes. Has all the desire to include 'we offer to you the bread and the cup' really been an insistence that a particular *metaphor should gain a centrality in our rites?* Certainly there is more hope of progress if anglo-catholics look at negotiable ways of expressing their doctrine. And evangelicals would be pleased to help.[4]

However, long-standing controversies are not the whole of our agenda. We turn to more tractable matters.

2. The Centrality of the Eucharist

The Assize Judges who listened to Keble in July 1833 were attending Morning Prayer, as were the vast majority of other Anglican worshippers throughout the country that Sunday morning. The

---

[1] Edited by Charles Walker (J. T. Hayes, London, 1868), p.106.
[2] *Ibid.* p.136. See also Question 345: 'Why is the priest to say [The Prayer of Consecration] "standing before the" altar?—Because this is the position of a sacrificing priest . . .'
[3] Rowan Williams *Eucharistic Sacrifice: The Roots of a Metaphor* (Grove Liturgical Study No. 31, 1982).
[4] See, for example, the Appendix 'Eucharistic Sacrifice—Some Interim Agreement' in *Growing Into Union*.

reformers' ideal of a weekly communion at which all would devoutly and sincerely partake had failed to make significant headway against the sheer weight of non-communicating inertia which had been the legacy of the Middle Ages. It is highly likely that many of the lower classes in particular never attended or received holy communion. Archbishop Secker of Canterbury had noted in his charge of 1741 that
> 'Some imagine the sacrament belongs only to persons of advanced years or great leisure or high attainment in religion, and is very dangerous for common persons to venture on'.[1]

Not only were the people unwilling to communicate, but the rite itself was infrequently celebrated. At the end of the eighteenth century and in the first part of the nineteenth, four communion services a year seems to have been the norm in a majority of praishes (and even this was a relatively recent improvement on the custom of thrice yearly celebrations at Christmas, Easter, and Whit.).

In contrast, however, the Tractarians learned from their Prayer Books that the Church of England made provision for, and thus presumably expected, a service of communion on *every* Sunday and on a number of Saints' Days as well. They were not of course the first to make this discovery. It is one of the ironies of liturgical history that 'Sacramentarians' had been one of the terms of abuse hurled at Wesley and the other early leaders of the Evangelical Revival when they insisted on receiving communion weekly. In fact the reasons which the early Tractarians gave for wanting to introduce a weekly eucharist into the life of the church were remarkably similar to those of their evangelical predecessors.[2] Both groups saw it as implicit in the dominical institution, both believed it to be the practice of the primitive church and of historical Anglicanism, and both evangelicals and Tractarians believed that the believer fed on Christ in the sacrament:
> 'The Sacrament of the Lord's Supper, professing as it does to feed us with the Bread of Life, and to make us spiritual partakers of the Body and Blood of Christ, ought, one would think, in all reason to form the most prominent feature in the worship of the faithful; to be dwelt on as the sure and abiding pledge of God's love, and sought for earnestly, if possible, as the daily, or at any rate, the weekly sustenance of souls hungry and thirst after righteousness.'

The words sound like the early Wesley, they are in fact those of Hurrell Froude.[3]

Why did the Oxford movement succeed in establishing a widespread weekly eucharist where the reformers and Evangelical Revival had failed? Certainly by 1967 many Anglican evangelicals were prepared to acknowledge that their own tradition had been impoverished by the

---
[1] Quoted in A. Russell, *The Clerical Profession* (S.P.C.K., London, 1980)), p.102.
[2] The common ground and parallels are explored more fully in T. Dearing, *Wesleyan and Tractarian Worship* (Epworth Press/S.P.C.K., London 1966).
[3] *Remains* II:I, 10f. Quoted in A. Hardelin, *The Tractarian Understanding of the Eucharist* (Uppsala, 1965), p.273.

relative neglect of the sacrament and found themselves admitting 'that we have let the sacrament be pushed to the outer fringes of Church life, and the ministry of the Word be divorced from it. Small communion services have been held seemingly at random, often more than one on a Sunday and the whole local Church seldom or never comes together at the Lord's Table . . . We determine to work towards the practice of weekly celebration of the sacrament as the central corporate service of the Church.'[1]

However, the connection between the Tractarians' desire for a weekly congregational communion and the parish communions of today is not a direct one. In between lie the years (between about 1880 and 1960) when much of anglo-catholicism followed a vastly different ideal. Rome, not the primitive church nor the provisions of the Prayer Book (not even in their most catholic interpretations), became the measure of all things—and Rome did not have general communion. So a High Mass replaced Morning Prayer at 11.00 a.m., but the anglo-catholic who wished to receive the sacrament had, like his evangelical neighbour, to get out of bed early and go to the 8 o'clock celebration.[2] In fact, although they may be tempted to claim it as one of their achievements now,

> 'Anglo-Catholics in the 1920's and 1930's continued to oppose the idea of the Parish Communion, stressing the importance of the Sung Mass at 11.00 a.m. when the sacrifice was offered and none should communicate.'[3]

Some anglo-catholics like Bishop Gore had attacked this non-communicating attendance as early as 1901[4], but it was not until Vatican II's stress on the importance of the faithful receiving at mass, that the hard-core of anglo-catholicism performed a *volte-face* and accepted the idea of a general communion as the main act of worship. Pius XII had slightly earlier relaxed the rule about fasting communion, and that made the changes easier.

Given that evangelical and anglo-catholics have to a considerable extent converged on a parish communion, are both equally satisfied with the achievement? The answer is that many are not, and rightly so. There have been casualties and new problems.[5] A couple of examples must suffice here.

---

[1] *Keele '67* (Falcon, London, 1967) para. 76. Ten years later this determination seems to have faltered somewhat: 'We are equally divided whether we should reaffirm . . . that the main church meeting on Sunday should be eucharistic in its worship.' (*The Nottingham Statement*, (Falcon, London, 1977) para. F3(c).
[2] The new emphasis on the discipline of fasting largely influenced the hour at which the sacrament was received. Total abstinence from midnight was widely urged among anglo-catholics following Roman practices.
[3] P. J. Jagger, *A History of the Parish and People Movement* (Faith Press, Leighton Buzzard, 1975) p.16.
[4] Quoted in P. J. Jagger, *op. cit.*, p.12.
[5] Infant Communion, which may well cause the greatest degree of heart-searching, is discussed in the next chapter.

ANGLO-CATHOLIC WORSHIP: AN EVANGELICAL APPRECIATION AFTER 150 YEARS

The sermon has been a noticable casualty in many churches. The mid-morning timing of the service, the wide age-range of the congregation, the time needed to administer communion to relatively large numbers (especially when laypersons are not used for this—and it is only very recently that they have been used freely): these have all combined to the shortening and simplifying of the sermon. Evangelicals have long protested at this undervaluing of the preaching of the Word. 'Five-to-ten-minute sermons squeezed into the Holy Communion service *will not do*' asserted Dr. Coggan[1], and many anglo-catholics have agreed with him. Back in 1937 when he contributed the chapter 'The Liturgical Sermon' to Hebert's *The Parish Communion*, M. R. Newbolt warned that 'any priest, who from the pulpit gives to the faithful, not the word of God, but his own speculations, is guilty of nothing less than sacrilege'[2], and implies that twenty minutes will be the length of the sermon. Despite much talk of alternative methods of communication and learning, the sermon is not going to be replaced, and its quality remains a matter of concern.

An equally serious casualty, and one which may prove much harder to remedy, is the people's preparation for communion. In *Durham Essays and Addresses* Michael Ramsey warned that a result of general communion could be a loss of 'communion as a responsible and dreadful act on the part of the individual'.[3] The last two decades which have seen the flowering of parish communions have also seen a great decline in the traditional disciplines of preparation. Catholics and evangelicals who cared enough about communion to make the effort to go to 8 o'clock were also likely to have put in some private spiritual preparation as well. In theory a 10.00 a.m. communion service should allow much more time for one's own preparation; in practice a lie-in, a full breakfast, preparing the dinner, getting the children ready, and a quick look at the Sunday papers[4] are often the activities which dominate the hour immediately before the service begins. Nor is there always much time for private prayer of any intensity in the service itself. The hum of conversation has replaced the awed silence before it begins and the fact must be faced that the presence of young children may seriously impair adult concentration.[5]

These are merely the problems that beset the 'regulars': the centrality of the eucharist presents problems for the 'fringer' or occasional visitor

---

[1] F. D. Coggan *Stewards of Grace* (Hodder and Stoughton, London, 1958) p.91.
[2] A. G. Hebert (ed.) *The Parish Communion* (S.P.C.K., London, 1937) p.210. (Newbolt is quoting Bossuet).
[3] A. M. Ramsey *Durham Essays and Addresses* (S.P.C.K., London, 1956) p.20.
[4] And now Breakfast TV!
[5] This raises the question as to whether children who have been at their own instruction during most of the service should rejoin the adult congregation in time to go up to the rail with their parents to be blessed. My own view is that the influx of young children, anxious to show the drawings, etc., that they have done in Sunday School can frequently shatter the mood of reverent approach to the Table that has been built up by the Ministry of the Word, the Intercessions, Confession and Humble Access. This is also the view of Michael Hocking (*A Handbook of Pastoral Work* Mowbrays, London, 1977) p.18: '... parents have a right to peace and quiet and so do the other communicants ...'

too. To take but one example: the fact that baptisms now frequently take place in the communion service brings a steady number of uncommitted relations, friends of the family (and even parents and godparents) to the rail, some of them having clearly forgotten (if they ever knew) what to do with the bread and wine.

A feeling that something must be done to ensure a devout and proper use of the sacrament seems to be becoming an important theme in current anglo-catholic renewal. Some of the loudest applause in the Loughborough Conference in 1978 was for a young layman with a
> 'fervent plea . . . for the recovery of the disciplines of fasting, fasting communions, frequent and regular confession, frequent and well-prepared communions.'[1]

In his book *Signs of Glory*, written in preparation for the 1983 Loughborough Conference, Richard Holloway also warns strongly about the dangers of over-familiarizing the eucharist:
> 'perhaps the old prayer manuals, with their lengthy preparations for Mass and thanksgiving after Mass, overdid it a bit, but they were overdoing an instinct that was entirely appropriate. We need to discover some of the joy and awe our fathers in the faith had, as they fought to have the Mass at the centre of the Church's life.'[2]

One of the reasons that evangelicals resisted the parish communion was fear of herding the unconverted or unprepared to the sacrament: clearly both they and anglo-catholics perceive here a very real need; is it too much to hope that it could become an area of constructive co-operation?

3. Doing the Eucharist

The heirs of the Tractarians have not of course merely reinstated the eucharist as the main service on Sunday mornings, they have also profoundly affected *how* it is done and *when* it is done on other occasions.

As to *how*, the issue of ceremonial is dealt with elsewhere in this volume, but one point needs making here. Ceremonial usage often betrays how little anglo-catholics have adapted to new (or rediscovered) theological insights. Rite A, for example, enshrines Dix's Four-fold Shape (albeit in a corrected form)—elements are 'taken' *before* the Great Thanksgiving and it is the whole prayer that 'consecrates', yet in many churches (including it must be admitted, evangelical ones too) there is little sign that this has been understood. The mandatory Taking is widely neglected and solemn recitation, sanctus bells, manual acts, elevation and genuflection all conspire to perpetuate the notion that it is the dominical words that effect consecration. To take one further example: as recently as February this year the Church Union has published a Ceremonial Guide on Concelebration[3] which quite properly

---

[1] *Conference Report* (C.L.A., London, 1979) p.57.
[2] *op. cit.* p.68.
[3] Charles Smith, *Concelebration* (CLA, London, 1983). This 'Guide' largely ignores the recent work by two members of the Liturgical Commission, *Concelebration in the Eucharist* (GS Misc. 163, 1982)—let alone my own *Eucharistic Concelebration* (Grove Worship Series no. 82, 1982).

ANGLO-CATHOLIC WORSHIP: AN EVANGELICAL APPRECIATION AFTER 150 YEARS

questions the need or propriety of 'concelebrants' reciting the Words of Institution together and yet still insists that Anglican clergy should do it that way. This kind of unhealthy double-think is one of the most infuriating and disheartening aspects of dialogue with anglo-catholics.

Turning from the manner in which the eucharist is to be celebrated, a brief look is necessary at the occasions on which it is appropriate to perform the rite. Two strands in contemporary thinking may be discerned. One suggests that the only proper locus for the eucharist is the weekly assembly of the (hierarchically ordered) people of God—the Lord's People at the Lord's Table on the Lord's Day. The other line of thought argues that the eucharist is in some sense the place 'where heaven and earth meet' and that to celebrate it in or for a particular occasion somehow brings the redemptive power of Christ to bear upon it.[1] This latter view found a moving defence in Dix's most purple of purple passages:

> 'Was ever another command so obeyed? For century after century, spreading slowly to every continent and country and among every race on earth, this action has been done, in every conceivable human circumstance, for every conceivable human need, from infancy and before it to extreme old age and after it... Men have found no better thing than this to do for Kings at their crowning and for criminals going to the scaffold... for the wisdom of (a) Parliament... or for a rich old woman afraid to die...'[2]

Intensely moving, but (dare one ask) is it right? Is it defensible to appropriate the sacrament for a particular 'cause'?[3] Is there not a danger of divorcing the sacraments from our ecclesiology? Anglo-catholics have encouraged all Anglicans into something of a 'chips with everything' mentality with regard to communion. The principle that saw it as appropriate at requiems and nuptials is easily extended, to synods, conferences, parish organizations and the like. However the predominant motive nowadays seems to be not so much that a celebration has an objective 'value' which will benefit the particular end, but an instinct that members of a group will find themselves more deeply committed to each other and their cause for having shared communion together. Does the fact that that instinct is often proved right suggest that the eucharist itself is in some sense capable of forming communities?

The issue of what is an appropriate eucharistic community brings us back to where the chapter started, namely to the local church at its weekly worship. Anglo-catholicism has contributed in large measure to the forces that have revolutionized that worship over the last 150 years particularly in its eucharistic forms; its challenge today is to rise to the problems, both practical and theological, created by that success.

---

[1] The *Church Times* of 8 January 1983 reported a 'Eucharist for Social Justice'. There have also been celebrations of communion outside the Greenham Common Air Base.

[2] G. Dix, *The Shape of the Liturgy* (Dacre/Black, London, 1945) p.744.

[3] I write with some hesitation, having insisted (and found it entirely right) that my wife and I (and not the congregation) should receive holy communion at our wedding.

2. '. . . THIS CHILD IS REGENERATE'
by Colin Buchanan

1. Baptismal Regeneration

Baptism in the pre-Tractarian Church of England was a necessary postnatal ritual which ensured that the existence of a child was duly registered in the parish records, and that a proper Prayer Book burial in duly consecrated ground was available if he or she should die. The Prayer Book taught that the infant, thus baptized, was regenerate, but the lax and latitudinarian church set little store by the inner change this implied. The Evangelical Revival had tended to find baptism an embarrassment, the Calvinists sheltering under the doctrine of election, and the Arminians (particularly John Wesley) teetering towards saying that a man born again in baptism might lose the benefit and still need as an adult to be born again (again).

Baptism was no embarrassment to the Tractarians. They revelled in it. None could have bid higher the grace, the miracle, the wonder of this sacrament:

'In Pusey's mind . . . the battle for sacramental grace was a battle for continued belief in the revelation of God in Christ.'[1]

In Tracts 67-69, on baptism, the whole doctrine was set out at great length by Pusey, without concession to the eighteenth century's views, and with a total dependence upon the literal wording of the Prayer Book's rite for infant baptism without regard for any hedging of its meaning by the English reformers.[2] The doctrine found great favour, and was quickly to be found spread far wider than simply among the immediate disciples of Newman and Pusey.

However, it shortly ran into contention—and contention of a most colourful and headline-snatching character. In 1846 the Lord Chancellor nominated George Cornelius Gorham to Henry Philpotts, Bishop of Exeter from 1830 to 1869 (and then almost seventy years of age), for institution to the living of Bampford Speke. Philpotts already knew Gorham—a crabbed but learned opponent of what he called, in an advertisement for a curate, 'Tractarian error'. Philpotts insisted on examining Gorham about his doctrine of baptism, and did so over eight separate days in December 1847 and March 1848. At the end of this unprecedented exercise he declared Gorham to be in doctrinal error, because he would not assert that all infants baptized were *ipso facto* regenerated.[3] This threw the onus onto Gorham, and he first of all

---

[1] H. P. Liddon *Life of E. B. Pusey D.D.* (Longmans Green, London, 1894) Vol. I, p.348.

[2] The actual title of nos. 67-69 was *'Scriptural Views of Holy Baptism'*. No. 70 was *'Notes to the Scriptural Views of Holy Baptism'*. Also of interest is no. 82 (by Newman) *'Letter addressed to a Magazine on behalf of Dr. Pusey's Tracts on Holy Baptism'*.

[3] The whole story is well written up in J. C. S. Nias *Gorham and the Bishop of Exeter* (S.P.C.K. London, 1952). Gorham's own account of his interrogation by the Bishop is also available in *Examination before Admission to a Benefice by the Bishop of Exeter followed by Refusal to Institute on the Allegation of Unsound Doctrine* edited by the Clerk Examined George Cornelius Gorham B.D. (Hatchards, London, 1848). Nias' book contains very full bibliographical references.

appealed to the Court of Arches[1] summonsing the bishop to show cause why he would not institute him, and looking for an injunction from the court requiring to bishop to institute. Philpotts' defence was of course that Gorham was formally heretical and therefore could not be instituted. Thus a heresy trial happened in a back-to-front way—the plaintiff having his doctrine on trial, and the defendant being the one to bring charges of heresy. The Court of Arches heard the case in January and February 1849, and Sir Herbert Fenner Just delivered his judgment on 2 August 1849. The Bishop of Exeter was upheld in his refusal to institute. Meanwhile the parties of the Church of England were alerted. Marching and counter-marching, pamphleteering and posturing—all flourished. Evangelicals saw their whole existence within the Church of England as under threat if Gorham were defeated. Anglo-catholics rallied to Philpotts' cause equally naturally. But a crucial event in relation to the final stages of the controversy came with the publication of William Goode's massive and definitive work, *The Effects of Infant Baptism*.[2] In this, Goode demonstrated that the doctrine of Gorham was the doctrine held by the compilers of the Prayer Book, the doctrine expressed in all the other formularies of the Church of England, and the doctrine held almost without exception by all the leading divines of the Church from Cranmer till the period under review. Finally, he showed that the doctrine taught by Philpotts had arisen within the Church of England from a tract written by Bishop Mant and published by 'the Christian Knowledge Society' *in 1815*. This is before the Tracts, but it is contemporaneous with Philpotts' prime of life, and it clearly laid the groundwork for the acceptability of Pusey's Tracts when they came. Thus the doctrine now upheld by the Court of Arches was, in Anglican terms, an innovation!

Gorham was in any case not giving up. He appealed to the Judicial Committee of the Privy Council, then the highest court of appeal in ecclesiastical causes. The Judicial Committee reversed Fust's judgment in the Court of Arches, and found for Gorham. This was the Judicial Committee's understanding of the doctrine which it upheld as compatible with the formularies and as held by Gorham:

> 'That Baptism is a sacrament generally necessary to salvation, but that the grace of regeneration does not so necessarily accompany the act of Baptism that regeneration invariably takes place in Baptism; that the grace may be granted before, in, or after Baptism; that Baptism is an effectual sign of grace, by which God works invisibly in us, but only in such as worthily receive it—in them alone it has wholesome effect, and that without reference to the qualifications to the recipient, it is not in itself an effectual sign of grace. That infants baptized, and dying before actual sin, are certainly saved; but that in no case is regeneration in baptism unconditional.'[3]

---

[1] This is the Provincial Court of the Ecclesiastical Province of Canterbury.
[2] This book is 500 pages long, and it was first published in the middle of 1849. Goode was explicitly doing his research in order to relate it to Gorham's predicament, and he succeeded magisterially.
[3] Nias' *op. cit.* p.98.

'... THIS CHILD IS REGENERATE'

Thus were the evangelicals saved! And the anglo-catholics were shaken. This decision precipitated secession to Rome by Manning and Robert Wilberforce[1], as also by Badeley the Bishop of Exeter's advocate before the Privy Council. The finding had not, it should be noted, declared Gorham right and Philpotts wrong—it had merely asserted that *both* positions were compatible with the formularies. This was salvation to the persecuted evangelicals, but threatening to the self-confident assertions of the anglo-catholics.

Not all anglo-catholics followed the retreat of Manning, or the defiance of Philpotts.[2] One well worthy of mention here was J. B. Mozley. He had been a pupil of Pusey, living with him at the very time that Pusey's own writings on baptism were being produced.[3] But in later years, whilst still associated with the Tractarians, he reviewed the whole Gorham Judgment very coolly in *The Baptismal Controversy* and drew two conclusions:

> 'one, that the doctrine of the regeneration of all infants in baptism is not an article of the faith; the other, that the formularies of our Church do not impose it'.[4]

So the bitterness of the controversy came to an end—with the evangelicals paradoxically having secured a footing in the Church of England which has continually troubled their consciences ever since (that is, many have believed superficially—or even masochistically—that Philpotts had the right interpretation of the formularies!).[5] And perhaps we ourselves could now content ourselves with noting three things the two sides had in common, even while they seemed desperately divided:

1. Both sides assumed that all infants born in England should be and would be baptized—baptismal *policies* were still a hundred years away.

2. Both sides found themselves handling the question of benefits to the *individual* conveyed by baptism. Neither was able to think easily in a wider corporate or ecclesiological framework.

3. Both sides agreed that the first and obvious meaning of the baptismal liturgy in the BCP suggested invariable efficacy. This caused frustration to anglo-catholics when the opposite case was

---

[1] Robert Wilberforce, brother of Samuel and son of William, was Archdeacon of the East Riding, and prior to the Judicial Committee's judgment he had published his own *The Doctrine of Holy Baptism with Remarks on the Rev. W. Goode's 'Effects of Infant Baptism'*, in which he attempted to read back Philpotts' doctrine into earlier centuries of Anglican divines.

[2] This included breaking communion with the See of Canterbury (Nias *op. cit.* p.115), but it has since been restored.

[3] See Liddon *op. cit.* Vol. 1 p.338 and Vol. IV p.220.

[4] J. B. Mozley *The Baptismal Controversy* (Rivingtons, London, 1863) p.iv.

[5] cf. Nias *op. cit.* pp.155-6. See also the steps taken by the Free Church of England to remove 'Seeing . . . that this child is regenerate' (A. E. Peaston *The Prayer Book Tradition in the Free Churches* (James Clarke, Cambridge, 1963) p.83) and similar steps which were debated but not implemented in the Church of Ireland Prayer Book in 1878 (see the Preface to that Book).

favoured by the Judicial Committee, whilst still causing embarrassment to evangelicals who functioned superficially. The position of Gorham was *de facto* on the decline in the Church of England at the time, and, because it is sophisticated and needs cogent advocates, it has not been broadly held in the Church of England since. Evangelicals have lacked the interest in sacramental and liturgical theology to make inroads into others' thinking, and a mild catholicism has here, as elsewhere, become the norm of Anglican belief.

2. Baptism and Confirmation

We pass on to the next round of dissension—inevitably concerning confirmation. In the days of the Tracts no one could build much doctrine into the Prayer Book requirements of confirmation, because (it seems) the rite was very badly administered, and many in the land became communicants without ever being confirmed at all.[1] With the Sumners and Samuel Wilberforce a 'pastoral' use of confirmation came into fashion. And the second generation of anglo-catholics therefore inherited a more systematic practice, onto which it was easier to fasten their doctrine of the absolute necessity of confirmation, and the 'two-stage' division of benefits between baptism and confirmation. Thus:

> 'The gift of the new birth [sc. by water-baptism] is . . . to be followed as soon as possible by the gift of the Spirit's indwelling [sc. by confirmation].'[2]

This school seems to have begun in the 1880s.[3] It went beyond Rome in the distinctive character of its teaching about confirmation. It appealed to the 'confirmation rubric' in the BCP to exclude free churchmen from communion.[4] It became the dominant school in the Church of England (and indeed in the whole Anglican Communion) from 1890 to 1970.[5] It affected the drafting of the 1927-8 'proposed'

---

[1] A useful history of the administration of confirmation in the Church of England is to be found in S. L. Ollard's essay 'Confirmation in the Anglican Communion' in *Confirmation or the Laying on of Hands: Vol. I Historical and Doctrinal* (S.P.C.K., London, 1926).

[2] A. J. Mason *The Relation of Confirmation to Baptism* (Longmans, London, 1891).

[3] The *fons et origo* is usually thought to be F. W. Puller *What is the Distinctive Grace of Confirmation?* (1880). The major work in that period was Mason *op. cit.* It is a remarkable contrast with Pusey's writing and thinking on baptism—in the whole of the four-volume *Life* of him there are virtually *no* references to confirmation at all—once to his own confirmation, once to that of a godchild, once a bare word that it is a 'means of grace'. There seems to have been no controversy about the rite, almost no *awareness* of it even, in the 1830s! And after Puller and Mason there were still anglo-catholics who were unhappy about 'two-stage' initiation, notably Darwell Stone in his *Holy Baptism* (Oxford Library of Practical Theology, Longmans, London, 1912).

[4] The first instance of this is usually reckoned to be the protests at Dean Stanley's 'Revisers' Communion' in 1881 (though the matter was there complicated by the presence of a Unitarian). The full battle-lines were drawn with Weston's denunciation of the 'Kikuyu' communion of 1913, and most of the Church of England quickly fell to anglo-catholic practice. The Lambeth conference of 1920, in its 'An Appeal to all Christian People' seemed to add confirmation (especially as admission to communion) to the two sacraments and the historic episcopate which had been in the 1888 'Quadrilateral' and were being repeated in the 'Appeal'.

[5] This was not solely through inertia. After 1930 a second generation arose to follow Puller and Mason. They included Dix (hence the 'Mason-Dix' nomenclature), Thornton, Ratcliff, and J. D. C. Fisher.

'... THIS CHILD IS REGENERATE'

Prayer Book rite.[1] And as it became the norm of Anglicanism it distorted bishops' addresses at confirmation. Sermon after sermon taught that *this* is the sacrament of the gift of the Spirit—often creating experiential expectations which were not matched in the outcome.

It may be noted that the 'Mason-Dix' line also sowed the seeds for that uniting of baptism, confirmation, and communion which later came about in the liturgy of the Church of England. However, although (as the quotation from Mason opposite shows) the school of thought wanted them in one service (whether for infants or adults), yet the theological problem of the 'distinctive grace' of confirmation remained, and was indeed exacerbated by the need to write actual liturgical prayers around the confirmation, which would say *something* theological.

But the 'two-staging' has been on the decline in recent years. Theologically and liturgically it runs on momentum acquired during the eighty years of supremacy. Its head of theological steam died away around 1970, and is still falling. Lampe and Dunn and Whitaker refuted it at the academic level.[2] The General Synod in 1971-2 voted to change the Canons and allow free churchmen to receive communion in the Church of England.[3] The Liturgical Commission expressed doubt about the need to confirm those baptized as adults in 1977.[4] And the General Synod, at the time of writing, has just given a heavy endorsement to the concept of admitting children to communion prior to confirmation.[5] Each and every one of these milestones points to the fact of 'sacramental initiation complete in baptism'. Even the confirmation addresses of bishops have veered about. The onus of

[1] In the 1928 service the 'Samaritan' episode in Acts 8 is cited as the biblical warrant for confirmation—though it is only asserted that 'a special gift of the Spirit' is conveyed by it, and not the Spirit himself *simpliciter*. This service ran strong in bishops' affections till 1966, when it perished in the House of Laity.

[2] Lampe wrote first, in *The Seal of the Spirit* (Longmans, London, 1953)—running right against a tide in full spate. J. D. G. Dunn's *Baptism in the Holy Spirit* (S.C.M., London, 1970) demolished 'two-stage' theology from a scriptural point of view, and E. C. Whitaker, in his second edition of *Documents of the Baptismal Liturgy* (S.P.C.K., London, ²1970), and in his *Sacramental Initiation Complete in Baptism* (Grove Liturgical Study no. 1, 1975), made it clear that the early church had no such unanimity about the two stages as had been asserted by the 'Mason-Dix' brigade. These writers have not been answered.

[3] This change is *very* recent, yet has been virtually total in its effects. Baptized non-Anglicans are now guests at communion without confirmation, and without a mutter from any quarter that they are not properly initiated. Yet to go back only fifteen years would present a Church of England which had in 90% of its parishes come to believe that the 'confirmation rubric' excluded non-Anglicans and did so because episcopal confirmation was pre-requisite to being recognized as truly Christian. The *volte-face* reflects the changing *theological* mood.

[4] See *Alternative Services Series 3 Initiation Services: A Report by the Liturgical Commission* (GS 343) (S.P.C.K., London, 1977) pp.6-7, and my own *Liturgy for Initiation: The Series 3 Services* (Grove Booklet on Ministry and Worship no. 65, 1979) p.9.

[5] In this February 1983 debate the only contrary speeches were from anglo-catholics who would have preferred to bring down the age of confirmation, in order to ensure it still gave admission to communion, rather than admit the unconfirmed. The Synod asked its Standing Committee, by a vote of 228 to 104, to review the decision of July 1976 not to change the traditional pattern.

proof now lies heavily upon any who would assert that the 'primitive' pattern was a unified baptism and confirmation. Only the water-baptism has universal claims, and our theology today reflects it.

3. Liturgical Accoutrements

Anglo-catholicism today remains much influenced by 'Mason-Dix' (and has not formally distanced itself from Philpotts). However, there has been a great tendency to think far more *corporately* about baptism, and to affirm the baptismal gift in a way that does justice to this. In recent years, there has come too a concern for baptismal *policies*.[1] But the most recent endeavour—a controversial one—has been to force permission for anointing into the baptism and confirmation services in the ASB. The Liturgical Commission had maintained that no such proposal should come before there had been a debate on the significance of such use of oil. But the provision was put into the text at the Revision Committee stage in General Synod[2], and anglo-catholics stated they would vote against the whole service if it were voted out. This was followed up by including in the alternative calendar a Maundy Thursday arrangement for 'The Blessing of the Oils'.[3] The only element lacking was the centrepiece—an actual liturgical text for 'blessing' oils. The Commission finally produced a blessing text after the ASB was published at the same time as it produced services for use with the sick. The Synod then took the 'Blessing of the Oils' to Final Approval—and then rejected it.[4] Part of the reason for this seems to have been a lack of any theological rationale. There *may* have been a few partisans who thought they were shipping 'Mason-Dix' back in through the back door when it was being eased out of the front—but only a few. The point was generally pursued not as a theological requisite but as a kind of necessary cosmetic decoration to initiation—with primitive roots and Roman precedents, but still without much theological basis. Few parishes are using such anointing in initiation, and therefore its theological importance cannot be stressed. Yet to make cosmetic ceremonies important is to suggest that they are more than cosmetic.

Am I right in thinking that the generations of authors mentioned above have almost come to an end? What anglo-catholic writers on initiation today can match those of the past? And has the movement on this point run out of steam and simply converted to oil? All of us take initiation now far more seriously than we would have done a hundred years ago. That may represent a long-term triumph for Pusey and Wilberforce. But I suspect that on the central issues involved—whether 'Gorham' or 'Mason-Dix' or liturgical anointing—the Church of England is slowly, very slowly, shaking itself free of anglo-catholic policies which looked tempting, but in the last analysis were built more upon romanticism than on a foundation of either scripture or the early church or pastoral need.

[1] Indeed anglo-catholics are now often *more* principled about striving to ensure that the administration of baptism does give credible boundaries to the church than are many others. All credit to them where that is so.

[2] See ASB p.225 Note 3, p.226 Note 7, p.241 Note 3, and p.252 Note 2.

[3] See ASB pp.555-557.

[4] The voting was: Bishops 26-6; Clergy 131-49; Laity 101-61. The Laity stopped short of the two-thirds majority necessary—the first defeat for a proposed rite since the 1928/Series 1 confirmation went down in June 1966 (see note 1 on p.21 above).

3. 'SEVEN TIMES DAILY WILL I PRAISE YOU'
by David Cutts

This short quotation from the longest Psalm must have been very familiar to the Tractarians, for this was cited by Newman as the justification for what had become the hours for prayer. Indeed his argument is well-founded on scripture and, even though many modern scholars would question his reasoning, Newman was most concerned to assure his readers that the Roman Breviary followed the example of the apostles as far as was recorded in scripture.[1] It is important to recognize from the outset this clear desire to conform to biblical precepts. Critics of anglo-catholics have not always appreciated that.

Newman certainly needed strong grounds for presenting a case for the saying of the office since, as has been related elsewhere[2], this particular form of Christian worship was at a very low ebb during the early part of the last century. It seems that after an increase of interest in saying the office during the last part of the seventeenth and early eighteenth centuries the rest of that century brought a steady decline so that offices were virtually unknown as *daily* services. Of course the situation on Sundays was rather different, as we shall see later. But why were Newman *et al.* so keen to re-establish this particular mode of devotion as part of their vision for the English Church of the future? Several reasons could be suggested:

1. As already noted, the Tractarians were keen to act in obedience to scripture. Newman therefore believed that to say the office was to follow the fine example set by the apostles as well as literally to obey the Psalmist's teaching. Immediately this can be seen to be wanting as a serious attempt at exegesis. Did Newman really believe the daily office was what Psalm 119 is about? Of course it might be argued that the office is a continuation of the Jewish pattern of worship and therefore Newman's argument is reasonable. However recent studies, particularly by Paul Bradshaw[3], have questioned many of the assumptions made in the past about the nature and form of Jewish worship and therefore in turn the origin of the daily office.

2. The office was seen as a link with the prayer of the early church by Newman and this link was reflected in the revival of ancient office hymns some of which can be found in today's hymnbooks.[4] 'Early church' here does not of course refer solely to the church of the New Testament since the information about any regular daily prayer is limited and uncertain. It is rather that the early anglo-catholics were keen to base their worship on the church right up to the Middle Ages and thus 'early church' is being used in a very broad sense.

---

[1] J. H. Newman Tract No. 75 'On the Roman Breviary' quoted in the article by C. W. Dugmore on 'Canonical Hours' in J. G. Davies (ed.) *A Dictionary of Liturgy and Worship* (S.C.M., London, 1972) p.113.
[2] David Cutts and Harold Miller *Whose Office? Daily Prayer for the People of God* (Grove Liturgical Study no. 32, Nottingham, 1982) pp.20, 30.
[3] Paul Bradshaw *Daily Prayer in the Early Church* (Alcuin Club/S.P.C.K., London, 1981).
[4] See for example *Hymns Ancient and Modern Revised* nos. 11, 14, 15.

3. Newman's use of Psalm 119 referred to above was in the context of writing about the Roman Breviary, and it goes virtually without saying that the renewed interest in the office was partly stimulated by the Roman pattern of daily worship. This was not of course without its problems, including the sheer volume of the Roman office, but in contrast to the Anglican apathy it must have seemed very attractive and worthy of support.

4. Monastic communities had naturally (or rather very un-naturally!) faded away during the period of the dissolution in the sixteenth century. Now interest was picking up, with some of the above factors providing the impetus. In a sort of 'chicken and egg' relationship the offices and monasticism bolstered each other amongst the Tractarians. In particular Compline caught on (and not only amongst anglo-catholics) as a service to be said last thing at night. This obviously satisfied a pastoral need, since many Christians appreciate some sort of prayer at this time.

5. All these reasons are important (and were important to Newman et al.) but it is doubtful if the office would have stayed the course had it not been for the spiritual value that was found in it (and still is). We shall examine this later.

The effect of this regained concern for priests and others to say the office has not had a particularly marked impact on the revision of the liturgy during this century. The offices in the proposed book of 1928 were little different in style from 1662 and Prime and Compline were added only as part of the Appendix. I do not easily understand the inclusion of Prime and indeed I recently discovered a priest of the Catholic school who was totally unaware of it being there. It would be interesting to know if Prime has been used much. I have no doubt that Compline has made its mark.

Presumably part of the lack of change in the office is because the controversies of the last century did not affect the office. No-one particularly minded what was worn for offices, and the words contained nothing offensive to the most protestant of the clergy. The ASB provision for the offices has brought some change, though it is difficult to detect any alteration due to 'party' views. Of course there was the inevitable supporter of the Roman Breviary who encouraged everyone to go out and buy the then recently produced new Roman office. In reply George Timms reminded the Synod of the cost of this book (£35 then) which, judging by the voting, was enough to dissuade the assembly from examining the 'rival' further. In fact the voting on the Series 3 provisions for Morning and Evening Prayer was virtually unanimous, which must say something about the lack of contention.[1]

We now come to examine how the office is seen today in these circles. There are a number of points:

1. We have to ask the question as to how many catholics actually say the office, especially with the conflicting demand of a daily

---

[1] *Report of Proceedings* 5 February 1975 pp.139, 142.

mass. I suspect (and it is only a suspicion) that most, if not all, do, though not necessarily in church. A recent informal survey amongst local clergy (of all attitudes) indicated that most clergy do use the office as part of their prayer life, though some have given up trying to attract a congregation.

2. Part of this routine is in obedience to the Canon. In other words there is a sense of obligation in saying the office. This can acquire ridiculous ideas. I heard recently of a priest who before going away on holiday felt it necessary to run through the offices for the holiday period in advance so that they would be said!

3. This concept of obligation is related to the idea (which seems to be particularly prevalent amongst anglo-catholics) that the office is part of the work of the priest since he is praying for the people. This takes two forms. A priest is seen as praying for the people in the sense that anyone can pray (and particularly intercede) for anyone. But it is more than that because there is also the view that the priest is praying on behalf of the people. So the laity offer their work for God at their place of employment whilst meanwhile the priest offers the office in their stead. Before he prays the office he rings the bell to inform the parish that he too is now 'at work'. The priest is set aside to pray amongst other things—if the priest doesn't say the office, who will etc. . . .? This mediatory role of the priest is expressed for example in the writings of H. P. Liddon. He wrote 'In the daily office, self is almost, if not quite, dismissed, and he (the Priest) acts for others.' and later 'The Priesthood of the Great Intercessor has descended upon him'.[1]

4. There is a very real sense for many that there is a binding together with the church throughout both time and space. I referred above to the Tractarians' desire to link their office with that of Christians throughout the centuries and this is now manifest in the way that the office is seen as the Prayer of the Church (note the capitals). C. P. Hankey in his essay in A. G. Hebert's *The Parish Communion* argued strongly along these lines and illustrated the point with a delightful story of a monk and an Englishman.[2] Hankey had no doubt that corporate prayer led to private prayer and not *vice versa* and part of this 'corporateness' must be seen as being with unseen Christians. It is obviously difficult otherwise to feel at all 'corporate' in a cold lonely church building.

5. There is obvious value in the office *in itself.* As the Tractarians found, it is neither simply a matter of obligation, nor of prayer on behalf of the congregation, nor of being 'corporate'. Newman's view of this can be found in his excellent sermon on this topic[3], and it is interesting to find that he did not seem to have any great

[1] H. P. Liddon *Clerical Life and Work* (Longmans, London, 1895) pp.7f.
[2] C. P. Hankey in A. G. Hebert (ed.) *The Parish Communion* (S.P.C.K., London, 1937) chapter VI.
[3] *Newman's Sermons on the Daily Office.*

sense of the vicarious nature of the office discussed above, but rather valued it in itself for himself. Patently part of this value for the priest of saying the office (which is what Newman really imagined—he hoped others would come but did not seem very confident) is the daily reading of the Psalms and readings. The lectionary provides the opportunity for a systematic and objective covering of the Bible and this has much to commend it. Indeed the office is largely scripture and this will no doubt account for the lack of that controversy over contents and wording to which other services have been subjected.

Before concluding with an appreciation and criticism of this it should be noted that we have been talking so far about the *daily* use of the office, rather than a specifically Sunday use. The Sunday use of the office has declined considerably in recent years and this can certainly be attributed in part to the anglo-catholic movement with its emphasis on the mass. A kindred factor has been the parish communion movement, which can surely be seen as having led to the demise of Sunday mattins in many churches.

So how are we to regard the anglo-catholic view of the office, if there is such a specific view to be found? Firstly, I believe we are much indebted to Newman for his attempts to encourage the saying of the office once again. Many Christians and in particular many clergy, have found the office to be a great spiritual strength in many different situations and without the revival of the last century we should lack this.

Secondly, the sense of obligation that many anglo-catholics feel about the office can be a lesson to those evangelicals who, due to the subjective nature of their prayer lives, have found it hard to pray during difficult times. When the desire to pray is weak for whatever reason the sense of 'having to' pray can be a helpful drive. But it has to be said that this obligation can also become a 'stumbling block' since it can too rapidly lead to legalism. It is at this point that evangelicals have wanted to draw a line and remind everyone that we are not 'under law'.

The objectivity of the office can be also a strength, because the lectionary gives a balanced diet of scripture which the evangelical may lack in his 'Quiet Time'. On the other hand, the office can be too inflexible, and a legalistic attitude to the lectionary raises a question an evangelical might want to ask an anglo-catholic.

The real sticking-point however is the concept of saying the office on behalf of the congregation. In the end it depends on what attitude a priest adopts towards his own ministry and whether he believes he has a vicarious role. It is obviously desirable that a clergyman prays for his people and that he realizes he has the time and opportunity to pray that most (and it is only most) lay people lack. In that sense then it is part of his work, but most evangelicals do not wish to pursue this any further. Some anglo-catholics would be content to stop here too, and say that this is all there is to their view of their ministry in respect of the office. So be it . . .

4. 'MAGNIFY YOUR OFFICE'
by Michael Sansom

'More sinners have been converted by holy men than by learned men' wrote Thomas Wilson, bishop of Sodor and Man from 1698 to 1755. The reprinting of his *Meditations on his Sacred Office* among the Tracts is ample testimony to a sense of kindred spirit felt for him by Newman and his fellow labourers. Like him, they longed for a clergy characterized by holiness of living and longed for bishops who would pursue an equally vigorous policy not solely to resist the pressures of Erastianism but more to raise the quality of spiritual life and pastoral efficiency in the nation. In Wilson, too, they saw a bishop who was a guardian against heresy[1] and they longed for similar guardians.

That the Tractarians were strongly in favour of episcopacy scarcely needs to be said. They regarded it as a divinely ordained defence against heresy[2]; they regarded it as a *sine qua non* for the continued life and spiritual health of the church. But it is also true that the episcopate as it existed at the time gave them little ground for the confidence they vested in the office and when it came to heresy it could scarcely be said that the Church of England was in significantly better case than those churches which had dispensed with the apostolic succession at the time of the Reformation.[3]

It was not, of course the mere institution of episcopacy that was important to them. Indeed, they rejected as firmly the *bene esse* view of episcopacy as they did the neglect of episcopacy.[4] The note, however, sounded insistently, especially in the early Tracts, is that of the importance of the *office* of the bishop or, indeed, of the *office* of each who came within the apostolic ministry. To magnify the office is not necessarily to exalt the individual who bears it;[5] the ministry of the church does not claim the ear of the people on the ground of its wealth or its status, but solely on the ground of its office, the burden laid upon it by Christ, for the pastor is 'the Deputy of Christ, for reducing man to the obedience of God.'[6]

Such is the office, the responsibility and task laid upon the ministry in respect of the church; so when Newman urges his fellow clergy to magnify their office, he is urging upon them a seriousness of purpose of a self-effacing manner which stands in the same tradition as the message conveyed to Simeon by his portrait of Henry Martyn: 'Don't trifle, don't trifle'. This is wholly consistent with the tenor of the examination of candidates in the Prayer Book ordinal. Richard Nelson is rightly made to wonder with astonishment 'that after such a solemn dedication to the ministry, there should be such a thing as a careless or a wicked clergyman.'[7]

---

[1] Wilson was imprisoned following an appeal by his Archdeacon Horrobin, whom he had suspended for heresy.
[2] Tract 54 3
[3] *cf.* Tract 57.
[4] cf. Tract 7.
[5] Tract 17.
[6] Tract 4.
[7] Tract 12.

ANGLO-CATHOLIC WORSHIP: AN EVANGELICAL APPRECIATION AFTER 150 YEARS

Behind the concept of *office*, however, lies a great deal more than the apostolic commission of Matthew 28.19; hand in hand with apostolic 'commission' goes apostolic 'succession'. But there is more still, for it is clear that the Puritans felt the apostolic commission no less keenly than the Tractarians: they no less than the Tractarians would have assented to the description of the pastor as 'the Deputy of Christ for reducing men to the obedience of God'. Similarly, they acknowledged in practice a form of succession: Tract 15 draws attention to the insistence of Dissenters on the ordination of ministers by ministers.[1] What occasions the divide between Dissenting and Tractarian views is *episcopal* succession. In ordaining other presbyters, Dissenting presbyters had 'assumed a power which was never entrusted to them.'[2]

Thus, while ostensibly resting their case on the divine origin and so the priority of the apostolic *commission*, the Tractarians subtly transformed the issue into a question of apostolic *succession of an episcopal brand*. On this depends a lot more, for the Tracts insist that episcopal ordination is essential not first as a question of the order of the church but as a matter of sacramental integrity; thus the Church of England is 'the only Church in this realm which has a right to be quite sure that she has the Lord's body to give to His people.' What is certain, however, is that while they may invoke the Ordinal to offer testimony on the question of the character of the clergyman's life, they cannot invoke it to offer testimony on this; for while it (however questionably) traces the threefold ministry back to New Testament times and insists on the necessity of episcopal ordination, the nearest that it comes to explaining the necessity of episcopacy is in the rubric at the head of the deacons' and priests' services directing that the sermon shall dwell on the necessity of that order in the Church of Christ.[3] Impressive as the argument of the Tracts may be, it is not part of Anglican doctrine and indeed would have found very little support among Anglicans in the sixteenth and seventeenth centuries as even Darwell Stone was willing to admit.[4] Nor will repeated insistence make it Anglican doctrine.

There has also been regular resort to the Preface to the Ordinal, which refers to the purpose of the Ordinal, is to be used 'To the intent that these Orders may be continued, and reverently used and esteemed'. If 'these Orders' are 'continued' from the pre-Reformation era—and patently they are—then, on an anglo-catholic exegesis, they may be made to carry any amount of pre-Reformation understanding of priesthood with them. This however is to ignore the extent to which Cranmer's Ordinal itself remodels our understanding of the ordained ministry.

It should be noted that the emphasis upon episcopal ordination goes beyond second century understandings of 'succession' the earliest we have. Ignatius of Antioch lays great weight upon the office of the bishop, but says nothing about 'succession' (Jesus Christ is going to

---

[1] It ought to be added that in a few Dissenting circles deliberate attempts have been made to avoid all suggestion of a succession, even to omitting any laying on of hands.
[2] Tract 10.
[3] And this 'necessity' began in 1662, and did not extend to the office of a bishop!
[4] Cited by N. Sykes *Old Priest, New Presbyter* (Cambridge, 1957) p.211.

have to be the emergency successor to the see of Antioch when he is martyred!). Irenaeus of Lyon two generations later promotes the notion of succession in teaching office. But neither discusses the *method* of appointment or ordination. The claim of the Tracts thus went beyond apostolic commission to apostolic succession—and beyond apostolic succession to apostolic *transmission*.[1]

The issue sometimes finds expression in such a phrase as 'the grace of orders'. It is a pity that it is so rarely explained, as I suspect that there are many who simply do not understand what it means. No doubt, if pressed to elucidate, most anglo-catholics would do so in terms of absolution and the validity of the sacraments. In the phraseology of the ARCIC statement of 1973, the ministry of the ordained priesthood 'is not an extension of the common Christian priesthood, but belongs to another realm of the gifts of the Spirit'.[2] The grace of orders is a special gift of the Holy Spirit which others do not possess.

Putting a finger on what is amiss with this is not easy, but the practical outworking suggests that locating the error is a necessary task. Neither the Tractarians, nor, I am persuaded, many present-day anglo-catholics would want the church, to use Anthony Hanson's words, delivered bound hand and foot into the hands of the ministry[3], but that, in effect, appears to be the result. Long ago, Elliott-Binns identified clericalism as an effect of the Oxford Movement[4] and more recently Anthony Russell has drawn attention to the way in which 'liturgical specialization' gave the clergy the protective aura of professional status.[5] What is wrong with the argument is that it seems that the validity of the sacrament is being based exclusively upon the mechanics of episcopal ordination. The obvious response to this suggestion is 'No, that is just the point: it is dependent upon the Holy Spirit given to those who are ordained precisely so that they should perform this task'.

[1] This is most pointedly illustrated in J. M. Neale's hymn for Ember days, *Christ is gone up.* Verses 2 and 3 run as follows:

    'His twelve Apostles first he made
       His ministers of grace:
    And they their hands on others laid
       To fill in turn their place

    So age by age, and year by year,
       His grace was handed on;
    And still the holy Church is here,
       Although her Lord is gone.' (*A & M Revised* no. 470, *English Hymnal* no. 156)

This has it all!—tactual transmission, grace a transmissible 'stuff' separable from Christ, and the church linked to her Lord not by cleaving vertically by faith but by being 'graced' through the horizontal pipeline of 'stuff' from the first bestowal of it upon the apostles by their risen Lord. It may not be sung at ordinations (is it?), but it seems to have commended itself to even twentieth century hymnbook editors. It is embarrassing that J. M. Neale *actually* said what evangelicals have always thought anglo-catholics were saying.

[2] ARCIC, *The Final Report* (Catholic Truth Society and S.P.C.K., London, 1982) p.36.
[3] A. T. Hanson *The Pioneer Ministry* (S.C.M., London, 1961) p.139.
[4] L. Elliott-Binns *Religion in the Victorian Era* (Lutterworth, London, 1936) p.446.
[5] Anthony Russell *The Clerical Profession* (S.P.C.K., London, 1980) pp.100-110.

ANGLO-CATHOLIC WORSHIP: AN EVANGELICAL APPRECIATION AFTER 150 YEARS

The problem with the reply is that it stops too soon—for the danger of the argument is that in a strange way, having yielded responsibility into the hands of the Holy Spirit it takes it straight back into the hands of man—or the priest—as possessor of the gift. Moreover, it fails to locate the gifts adequately within a doctrine of the church. Consequently the effect of the doctrine is to place the presidency at the eucharist at the *functional* (instead of the *symbolic*) heart of the doctrine of ordination. But a priest is ordained not narrowly to preside at the eucharist but to exercise pastoral care in the church. Presidency of the eucharist is the proper concomitant of that pastoral care. The eucharist is the focal point of the church's worshipping life, and it is itself symbolic of the innermost character of pastoral care. There is a two-way traffic between eucharistic presidency and pastoral care. It is the pastoral nature of the office which is so carefully underlined by the ordinals of both the BCP and the ASB It is the eucharistic symbol which gives meaning and direction to pastoral care, but it is the practising of pastoral care which is the basis for presidency at the eucharist. Anglo-catholicism has all too often seemed to make the sacraments derivative from the valid ministry, and the church derivative again from the sacraments. This is exactly what has been at stake in reunion negotiations. The anglo-catholic programme, however, hedged with sophisticated reservations, has come across as 'First validate their ministry; then their sacraments will be acceptable; and that will ensure they have the right "notes" of the the church about them.' And 'validating' their ministry has not been easy when episcopal transmission of grace and office has been a *sine qua non* in discussion. A more healthy view (still incorporating an episcopal ministry at its heart) was near acceptance in the Covenant proposals. Many anglo-catholics did vote for such a 'recognition' within carefully defined limits when the General Synod responded to the Ten Propositions in 1978. But by 1982 the final proposals were felt by anglo-catholics to reveal a shift from the careful safeguards, and they went into opposition again.

It was interesting to observe the influences upon the new ASB ordinal. Clearly Ratcliff and other liturgical scholars wanted a *prayer* to be said over the candidates at the laying on of hands, and to get away from the medieval exhortation. Equally the 'whose sins you forgive' was doomed (it only appears in a gospel reading). The word 'presbyter' entered as an alternative (and thus an explanation) for 'priest'.[1] Some more catholicized ceremonial was implied in three of the Notes, two of them pushed in at revision stage in Synod; as e.g.:

> "It is appropriate that the newly ordained should be invited by the bishop to exercise their ministry in the course of the service."[2]

Note 7 concerns vesting and Note 8 the delivery of 'symbols' of office (over and above the Bible). I hope it will not seem perverse to say so, but it seems to me that while it is perfectly appropriate that the bishop should receive his pastoral staff as the symbol of *his* pastoral office (and somewhat regrettable that he does not go on to preside at the eucharist) it is not appropriate to give the presbyter a chalice and paten

---

[1] Interestingly, the word used by Newman in Tract 1.
[2] ASB p.338. It is of course impossible for new presbyters to *preside* (or for a new bishop to ordain).

unless it can be seen far more clearly that it *symbolizes* (rather than constitutes) *his* pastoral office.[1] Still less is it appropriate that he should take part in the highly questionable expedient of reciting the eucharistic prayer (either the president should say it alone or everyone—but everyone—should join in[2]). The quicker that such malpractice is abandoned, the better.[3]

Anglo-catholics have done much to make ordination services more suitably solemn occasions, but there also seems to me to be a danger of creating an atmosphere which is all too cosy, domestic, or churchy and is a very far cry from (for example) Tract 10 with its insistence on the office of a bishop in preaching, witnessing, and suffering. The ministry of the presbyter is presented as a liturgical ministry within the circle of the Christian fellowship. But there is far more to the pastoral care of the people of God, even if that responsibility is symbolized and focussed in the eucharist; the ASB puts it well:

> 'A priest is called by God to work with the bishop and with his fellow-priests, as servant and shepherd among the people to whom he is sent. He is to proclaim the word of the Lord, to call his hearers to repentance, and in Christ's name to absolve, and declare the forgiveness of sins. He is to baptize and to prepare the baptized for Confirmation. He is to preside at the celebration of Holy Communion. He is to lead his people in prayer and worship, to intercede for them, to bless them in the name of the Lord, and to teach and encourage by Word and example. He is to minister to the sick and prepare the dying for their death. He must set the Good Shepherd always before him as the pattern . . .'

A little later the words of the Prayer Book are recalled—the candidates are to be 'messengers, watchmen and stewards of the Lord' required

> 'to teach and to admonish, to feed and to provide for the Lord's family, to search for his children in the wilderness of this world's temptations and to guide them through its confusions, so that they may be saved through Christ for ever.'

The ordinal does not envisage any comfortable retreat into ecclesiastical housekeeping: if the *porrectio instrumentorum* or the *vesting* are to mean anything they ought to be seen as the stigmata as much as the privilege of the Lord's service, the cross as much as the crown. It is in this sense that evangelicals and anglo-catholics alike should be happy to acknowledge the call to 'magnify their office', the office of going into all the world to preach the gospel, making disciples of all nations, baptizing them in the name of the Father and the Son and the Holy Spirit, teaching them to observe all that Jesus has commanded. However powerful may be the apostolic succession as a symbol of the continuity of the church's faith and ministry, it is secondary to the apostolic commission and neither anglo-catholics nor evangelicals should lose sight of that, however different their ways may be.

---

[1] The prime requisite for a eucharist to take place is not a priest but a congregation!
[2] cf. J. R. K. Fenwick, *Eucharistic Concelebration* (Grove Worship Series 82, 1982) and *Concelebration in the Eucharist* (GS Misc 163, C.I.O., London, 1982).
[3] Other priests who join in usurp the right both of the president *and* of the congregation! See pp.15-16 above.

5. 'WHOSE SINS YOU FORGIVE, THEY ARE FORGIVEN'
by David Gregg

Any treatment of the subject of auricular confession and judicial absolution in the anglo-catholic tradition is bound to lead very quickly to the question, 'How Tractarian were the "Tractarians"?' It is true that the role of the clergy as mediators of forgiveness was emphasized from the start. In Tract 1, Newman appeals to the Ordinal to show that this is, in his mind, the foremost consequence of 'APOSTOLICAL SUCCESSION' and 'THE MINISTERIAL COMMISSION'; and in Tract 17, Archdeacon Harrison underlines this with his assertion that a 'Ministry of Reconciliation' is at the heart of the 'Commission', and that it is to the comfort of those who cannot quieten their own conscience that 'a duly commissioned Minister of God's Word [is] at hand.' Yet nowhere is there so much as a hint, even in the most likely places, of anything other than precatory *formulae* for absolution. In Tract 39, for instance, 'Bishop Wilson's form of receiving penitents' has only, 'May the gracious God give you repentance to life eternal etc.'; while in Tract 74 Presbyter Hammond's piece on the 'Power of the Keys' concentrates entirely on the general matter of governing the church. In the only other direct reference to the matter, in the same Tract, in the reproduction of Bingham's *Sermons on Absolution No. 2*, 'judicial' absolution is mentioned twice, once as a tentative possibility, and once as not part of the normal provisions of the church.[1] This absence of support for the *te absolvo* (and all that goes with it) is strongly reinforced by a positive matter. At the head of the list of recommended further reading in the Tracts—books cited which are held to commend the principles of the nascent movement—stands 'Bishop Taylor on Repentance.' And on the *form* of absolution. Jeremy Taylor, having traced the origins of the 'confessional' to within a few years of Aquinas, writes:

> 54a '... in the primitive church there was no such thing as a judicial absolution of sins used in any liturgy, or church, so far as can appear; but all the absolution of penitents which is recorded, was the mere admitting them to the mysteries and society of the faithful in religious offices, the sum and perfection of which is the holy sacrament of the Lord's supper.'[2]

Elsewhere, he is equally categorical. In the second part of his *Dissuasive from Popery*, in the section entitled 'Auricular Confession imposed without authority from God', he writes:

> '... it appears that in the ancient discipline of the church a deacon might reconcile the penitents if the priest were absent... and if a deacon can minister this affair, then the priest is not indispensably necessary, nor his power judicial and pretorial.'
> (Book 1. Sect. XI. para. 4)

Furthermore, in the *Rule and Exercise of Holy Dying*, he speaks with great relevance to a current controversy when he says:

> 'And they were vain disputes which were commenced some few ages since concerning the forms of absolution, whether they were indicative or optative, by way of declaration or by way of

---

[1] All this makes one wonder if Newman was being unwittingly prophetic in Tract 1, when he begins by saying, 'I conceal my name, *lest I should take too much on myself by speaking in my own person*'! (italics mine).

[2] Jeremy Taylor *The Doctrine and Practice of Repentance* Ch. X. Sect. IV).

'WHOSE SINS YOU FORGIVE, THEY ARE FORGIVEN'
sentence; for at first they had no forms at all, but they said a prayer, and . . . laid hands upon the penitent when they prayed over him, and so admitted him . . . ' (Ch. V. Sect. IV. para. 6)

It is evident from all this that the adoption of the secret confessional, penitential disciplines and judicial forms of absolution not only owed little to most of the authors of the 'Tracts' but were apparently implicitly condemned by them. Nevertheless, the altogether laudable emphasis on holiness and repentance engendered by the new movement quickly gave rise to expectations which *had* to be met. As Trevor Dearing so judiciously chronicles, it was penitents presenting themselves to Pusey, Keble and others, demanding the rights which the Prayer Book appeared to offer them, that led to the introduction of 'auricular confession' and all that went with it.[1] Pusey's own use of the confessional, with Keble as his 'ear', on 1 December 1846 set the seal on this development. In Anglican practice the emphasis was always put, and still remains, on the *guidance and advice* given to the penitent, rather than on the spiritual *direction* which was the emphasis in the Roman rule. But nevertheless the emergence of the practice owed much to the fashion of imitating Rome, and its establishment among the Tractarians must go down as yet another 'romantic' revival of a basically medieval innovation.

Of all the liturgical and sacramental influences of the Oxford movement, this has made the least impact on Anglican worship as a whole. Unlike the eucharistic practices, vestments, baptismal doctrines, revival of offices, architecture, etc., the confessional has remained a particularity of anglo-catholicism as such. And such influence as it has had is now diminishing. The trend in the Roman Catholic Church, following Vatican II, towards the (albeit infrequent and closely controlled) practice of 'general' absolution—despite the disavowals of it being an alternative to private confession—and the new emphasis on liberation and salvation rather than introspection, have reduced its centrality. The omission of the specific commission concerning 'binding and loosing', in the ASB ordinal, marks a *formal* diminution of its place in the Church of England too.[2] In the new *Tracts for our Times* the only direct treatment appears to be in the reprint of Halifax's essay of 1932![3] Indeed, the only evangelical comment that *his* contribution elicits is that his Tridentine sequence of contrition, confession, satisfaction, and absolution, is at variance with that of the reformers, which reverses the third and fourth of these.[4] It is more in keeping with the Anglican emphasis on 'guidance', rather than the directional imposition of a 'penance', to adopt the arguably more scriptural notion of subsequent amendment of life as that which gives 'satisfaction'.[5]

[1] T. Dearing *Wesleyan and Tractarian Worship* (S.P.C.K., London, 1966) pp.62f.
[2] *'Formal* diminution'—that is, on anglo-catholic premises that the charge to the ordinand in the BCP is a charge to hear confession and give absolution. Others would want to understand 1662 in the way they understand John 20.22-23.
[3] Tom Sutcliffe (ed.) *Tracts for our Times* (St. Mary's Annual for 1983, Bourne Street).
[4] Is not private auricular confession itself at marked variance with the principle of 'Reserve in Communicating Religious Knowledge' which Roy Porter identifies as the essential genius of the original Tractarians, in its opening essay?
[5] See my *Penance* (Grove Booklet on Ministry and Worship no. 53, 1977) pp.5f.

ANGLO-CATHOLIC WORSHIP: AN EVANGELICAL APPRECIATION AFTER 150 YEARS

I have acknowledged elsewhere my own indebtedness to the anglo-catholic movement, for the tenacious preservation of an aspect of Christian life and experience on which I, along with many evangelicals, have been gravely 'missing out'.[1] And I feel keenly the sentiment of S. T. Bindoff when he says of a similar 'divide' in a different age:

'There were not lacking [those] who knew what they fought for, and loved what they knew, and whose part in it lifted this struggle far above the plane of power politics. They were a small company, and a tragically divided one. For they fought under hostile banners, and in their zeal mistook one another for the enemy.'[2]

Even if I have made out my case here, I ask forgiveness of my anglo-catholic brothers and sisters whom I have also sometimes mistaken for the enemy! And this essay could have terminated appreciatively, except that I write scarcely a week since the General Synod failed, by a blocking minority in the House of Laity, to approve a *Form of the Reconciliation of a Penitent* which would have enshrined, for the first time in post-Tractarian liturgy, the medieval romanticism *te absolvo*. An initial scrutiny of the proceedings during the debates suggests that the theological case against it was never sufficiently communicated. We have a short breathing-space. I conclude with an appraisal, and a plea, from one evangelical standpoint:

1. We might concede *all* the points about the contents of the BCP, its ordinal, the traditions of the church, the attitude of the reformers etc., concerning a judicial absolution yet never get to the nub of the matter; What do the scriptures say?

2. If we address ourselves to *that* point we observe (as did the Bishop of Salisbury in the Canterbury Convocation) that there is a unanimous tradition, extending to the words of Jesus himself, that only the *passive* form ('Your sins *are forgiven,* you are absolved') can preserve adequately and unequivocally the truth that it is God alone who is the 'forgiver'. Those who take the scriptures as their primary authority have no ground for 'speaking in my own person' (to borrow Newman's phrase!)

3. Indeed, the reprise to Tract 1 leads to a final observation, and the plea. The Tract is 'respectfully addressed *to the clergy*', and this highlights a residual suspicion that will have to be either admitted or allayed, that a hidden agenda lies behind the *te absolvo* lobby, namely that the formula heavily reinforces—nay, even epitomizes— the Tractarians' prime equation that it is the *clergy* who are the only legitimate heirs to Christ's ministerial commission. May I plead with my anglo-catholic friends to recognize that find this is at best 'not proven' and at worst a dangerous distortion, and that, if they press the point, they may shatter the Church of England we all love.

To parody Tract 90:
'The Elizabethan Confession was drawn up with the purpose of including *Protestants;* and Protestants now will not be excluded.'

[1] *Penance* p.3.
[2] S. T. Bindoff *Tudor England* (Pelican, 1950) p.99.

6. 'THE BEAUTY OF HOLINESS'
by David Parkes

The state of Church Architecture in 1833
The industrial revolution gave rise to immense growth of the towns of Lancashire and Yorkshire and the industrial Midlands, and of London itself. The Church of England did little in the earlier years of this growth to respond and the new population was either totally un-churched, or left to the less cumbersome evangelistic strategy of Methodism. An urgent need to build was recognized after the war with France ended in 1815. The Church Building Society was formed in 1818, and in various Church Building Acts £1.5 million was voted by Parliament for building churches. Much more was raised locally by private subscriptions.[1]

The churches which resulted are called 'Commissioners' Churches', or popularly 'Waterloo Churches'. There were 214 in all; to this day they stand black and four-square in the middle of mill towns from the Mersey to the Tees, in Birmingham and the Black Country.

Many of the Commissioners' churches are in classical style, but more than half are Gothic, for the Gothic Revival had become respectable since the early romantic essays of the later eighteenth century. Their plan is, however, in complete contrast to the later Gothic revival; they are galleried preaching halls, with a small extension to the east for the communion table, but with none of the arrangements which post-Tractarian ceremonial propriety required. Many have since acquired eastern choir-stalls and raised sanctuaries, but this was not the original arrangement. The Gothic style of these churches followed that of the fifteenth century, later known as 'Perpendicular', rather than the fourteenth century 'Decorated' style followed by Victorian architects.

Gothic Architecture and 'Catholic' worship
The early leaders of the Oxford movement were neither 'ritualists' in the later sense, nor were they great enthusiasts for the Gothic revival. Newman, for instance, had purely utilitarian views on church architecture.[2] There is a dull essay on architecture in Froude's *Remains*, but most of it could have been written forty years earlier.

The view arose quite soon after the pioneers, however, that the only tolerable architectural setting for 'catholic' Christian worship was the Gothic style of the mid-fourteenth century. The most prominent early prophet of this view was Augustus Welby Pugin (1812-1852) who joined the Roman Catholic church as early as 1834. Much of his work was done for Roman rather than for Anglican clients, but it had a profound influence in Anglican catholic circles.

Pugin was a great romantic. His view of the middle ages, and of their church life, was an unreal one, and his disappointment with nineteenth century catholicism and its aesthetic appurtenances was great. 'What's the use', Pugin is quoted as saying, 'of decent vestments with such

---

[1] Further on this, and on much in this essay, see Basil F. L. Clarke *Church Builders of the Nineteenth Century* (S.P.C.K., 1938).
[2] cf. T. Mozley, *Reminiscences*, vol. 1, p.345.

priests as we have got? Why sir, when they wear my chasubles they don't look like priests, and what's worse, the chasubles don't look like chasubles.'[1] Pugin's drawing of proposed buildings are powerful and evocative. The results are, by contrast, a little stiff and disappointing, even including Ushaw College chapel, one of his finest works.

'Ecclesiology'

The Cambridge Camden Society was founded in 1839 by J. M. Neale and Benjamin Webb, for the 'study of Gothic Architecture and Ritual Arts', a study for which the word 'Ecclesiology' was coined.[2] This was not simply an architectural or artistic study. The ecclesiologists thought that the layout and details of medieval churches had a hidden inner mystical meaning. It wished to unveil this esoteric significance, and to invest new churches with it. In 1841 the society began a periodical called *The Ecclesiologist* which continued until 1868, and exerted a profound influence, especially in its early years.

The position of the Ecclesiologists accorded exactly with the views of the Tractarians in matters of churchmanship, as may be seen:
'The most important requisite in erecting a church is that it be built in such a way that the Rubricks and Canons of the Church of England may be consistently observed, and the Sacraments rubrically and decently administered. But how can the chancel "remain as it hath done in times past", when there is no Chancel whatever? How can the Minister "baptize publickly at the stone Font", such Font standing "in the ancient and usual place", when, if it did stand so, he would be so enclosed by galleries, that most surely he would not be seen or heard?'[3]

In 1843 Neale and Webb published a translation of a thirteenth century work, the *Rationale Divinorum Officiorum* of William Durandus, Bishop of Mende. The interest which this has for us lies not in the original work but in the very long introduction by these two leading ecclesiologists, which gives an extended exposition of Camdenian doctrine as then held. An architect must be a devout catholic churchman. He must design nothing but churches, and in nothing but the 'middle pointed' (fourteenth century) style. There is a long dissertation on symbolism, much of which is rather far-fetched, and actual examples are given. Anything three-fold in ancient churches symbolizes the Trinity, as the division into nave, chancel, and sanctuary; or the arrangement of arcade, triforium, and clerestory; as well as any grouping of three windows, three steps, and the like. Octagonal fonts symbolize regeneration, because the day of resurrection (the first day) is also the eighth. A cruciform plan symbolizes the atonement. Windows symbolize Christ the Light of the World; a circle above a triple window symbolizes the crown of the King of Kings. A triple lancet joined by a hood moulding symbolizes the unity of the Godhead; two windows so joined, the two Natures of Christ, and so on, and so on. A protestant conventicle is then compared

---
[1] B. Ferrey, *Recollections of Pugin*, p.112.
[2] The name of the society was changed in 1846 to 'The Ecclesiological Society'.
[3] *The Ecclesiologist*, vol 1, no. 1 (2nd impression).

with a catholic church; everything in the protestant building symbolizes 'spiritual pride, luxury, self-sufficiency, and bigotry'. The peroration of this introduction works up a fine romantic enthusiasm for the glories of catholic architecture. Durandus proves to be a worthy thirteenth century ancestor of the Ecclesiologists. One quote can give the flavour:
> 'The towers are the preachers and prelates of the Church, which are her bulwark and defence . . . The pinnacles of the towers signify the life or the mind of the prelate which aspireth heavenwards. The cock at the summit of the church is a type of preachers.'

—the implication to which we are irresistibly drawn is that some such preachers need to come down to earth a little.[1]

We should here mention another prolific writer on Gothic architecture, who was probably ultimately more influential even than the Ecclesiologists: John Ruskin (1819-1900). When we turn from the writings of the Ecclesiologists to, for instance, his *The Seven Lamps of Architecture*, we find much that is familiar, especially in the fundamental assumption that architecture has a moral and spiritual as well as a simply artistic significance. But Ruskin was no Ecclesiologist. He was a convinced protestant with little sympathy with anglo-catholicism, yet with a deep love for Gothic architecture. Much that Ruskin said the Ecclesiologists agreed with, but there were two important contributions which he made which set him apart from them. first, that he dissociated Gothic architecture from popery in the popular mind; and secondly, that he introduced a welcome broadness of understanding of Gothic architecture outside Britain; the early Ecclesiologists were rather insular in outlook and experience.

Some architects and their work

The practical application of some of these matters can best be understood by considering some of the work of three actual architects. I am aware of the dangers. Many will say 'Why include A and not B?'

About the inclusion of Sir Gilbert Scott (1811-1878) there can be little argument, since no architect of the Gothic revival was either so respected in his own time or so prolific. A grandson of Thomas Scott, the great evangelical commentator, he was himself a man of profound personal faith, as is evident in his autobiographical *Personal and Professional Recollections*. He is perhaps best described as an 'evangelical catholic'. He was sufficient of a protestant to welcome the commission to design the Martyrs' Memorial in Oxford, and he offended the Ecclesiologists by designing a church in Hamburg for Lutheran 'hereticks'—almost worse than his designing workhouses, lunatic asylums, and railway stations! Yet he was profoundly influenced by Webb and Pugin, and his religious as well as his artistic attitudes (if, indeed, they are separable at this time) reflect those influences.

Scott's work is absolutely typical of the period. Indeed, one of the reasons why we tend to find his churches so dull by contrast with those of, for instance, Butterfield or Pearson, is that he set the style which

---

[1] Willielmus Durandus, *Rationale Divinorum Officiorum*, translated J. M. Neale and B. Webb (Cambridge, 1843) quoted in Clarke, *op. cit.*

ANGLO-CATHOLIC WORSHIP: AN EVANGELICAL APPRECIATION AFTER 150 YEARS

innumerable other architects followed, and therefore, whereas a Butterfield church is unmistakeable, be it in central London, agricultural Oxfordshire, or a Durham mining village, a Scott church might be by any competent run-of-the-mill Victorian architect.

The detail is strictly fourteenth century 'middle pointed', though with a stiffness and 'primness' which is peculiarly Victorian. The plan differs a little, however, from what was typical then. The Victorian chancel is wider and more spacious but not so long as the typical mediaeval chancel. The 'high altar' is more visible, and the chancel stalls more spacious, since they are required for a surpliced choir.[1] Instead of a side chapel or chapels there is perhaps a high and wide organ chamber to one side (containing an organ with no proper case as such above the level of the impost, but a decorative row of elaborately painted pipes). The nave, which would be largely unfurnished in a medieval church, is filled with what we call pews, which at the time were called 'benches' by contrast with the high box 'pues' deplored by the Ecclesiologists, and there is a large pulpit to one side of the chancel arch. Under the benches is a wooden floor, and the rest of the flooring is mainly of encaustic tiles (where the fourteenth century would largely have used stone flags). Later generations have covered the tiles with carpet. Scott's churches are largely English, both in detail, and in their square, not apsidal, east end, and in the proportions, which are wider in proportion to their height than is typical of churches following continental, particularly French, models.

William Butterfield (1814-1900) is the architect associated above all with the exploitation of constructive colouration. His churches are aggressive riots of colour, in brick, mosaic, and coloured stone. Butterfield was a High Churchman of exemplary piety, and would not build other than ecclesiastical buildings, and the sanctuaries of his churches are laid out spaciously in a way that lends itself to the elaboration of anglo-catholic ceremonial. Butterfield did not, however, provide side-chapels, and resisted the introduction of side-altars in his churches.[2] All Saints' Margaret Street, which with its predecessor, the 'Margaret Chapel', has been a centre of anglo-catholic worship since the 1840s, was designed by Butterfield, and was supposed to be the Ecclesiologists' model church.

John Loughborough Pearson (1817-1898) was born in Durham, and later described Durham Cathedral, particularly the nine-altars chapel, as having had a strong early formative influence on his ideas. Pearson is incomparable in his execution of ribbed vaulting. His churches provide fascinating vistas of intriguing complexity, through processional paths and side chapels well devised for the full elaboration of the anglo-catholic ceremonial of the latter part of the century. The early Ecclesiological dedication to 'middle pointed' style has now gone. Pearson's churches owe more to the thirteenth than to the fourteenth century in their inspiration: but they are not slavish copies of anything.

---

[1] See pp.45, 48 below.
[2] Butterfield is said to have been very angry when a side chapel was introduced into Keble College Chapel, Oxford, by raising the organ into a loft, and this work had to be done by another architect.

'THE BEAUTY OF HOLINESS'

Restoration and furnishing

Not only were great numbers of new churches built by the Victorians, but old churches were 'restored'. In many cases the structural state of the church was bad, but in many others restoration was carried out primarily to bring the structure into line with new notions of ceremonial propriety. In the process, much ancient and beautiful work was destroyed, or rendered unrecognizable.[1] Box-'pues' were anathema, and were replaced by benches. Chancel arches were often enlarged, and chancels filled with ugly choir-stalls. West galleries which had formerly accommodated singers and instrumentalists were removed, and organs crammed into side-chapels or specially built organ-chambers off the chancel. Three-decker pulpits were replaced. The arrangements at the east end were re-ordered, with the right number of steps in the right places. Gaudy tiles and other coloured materials were applied. Many of the wall paintings and stencilled texts which the Victorians introduced into restored churches have since been removed.

The new and restored churches required appropriate ornaments; quite apart from vestments, the provision of ecclesiastical furnishings and nick-nacks of one kind or another became something of a 'growth industry' in the nineteenth century: silverware and brassware, candlesticks, crosses, ironwork, statues, embroidery, woodwork, tiles, stained glass, organs, and bells, were made in a profusion which has not been known before or since. The techniques involved were not new, though new mechanization was applied to many of them. Some of the suppliers were old firms, but many others sprang up.

Wider effects of the Gothic Revival

The Gothic revival spread far beyond the building and restoring of churches for anglo-catholic worship, and the layout and furnishing of the Ecclesiologists have become accepted as Anglican custom.

These things spread overseas also. The Camden Society was involved at an early stage in the production of designs for churches in New Zealand. For these, they proposed a Norman style, which they did not approve in England, for 'as the work will be done by native artists, it seems natural to teach them first that style which prevailed in our own country'—presumably that they might go on spontaneously to develop their own 'first pointed' and 'second pointed'—and stop there.[2]

New Zealand did in fact later develop its own indigenous style of 'Wood Gothic'. Gothic architecture spread throughout the British empire; nowhere is it so inappropriate, perhaps, as in India, where an English suburban Victorian church implies that Christianity is the alien importation of a foreign culture, a hindrance to the gospel.

A quaint example of wooden Gothic is to be found at Balestrand on the Sognefjord in Norway. The English church in Balestrand looks at first glance as if it is a typical local Norwegian church—but look again, and it is in fact the interpretation by a Victorian English architect's office of what an indigenous Norwegian church ought to be.

---

[1] May we take warning in our own generation, perhaps especially in our own re-ordering of 'worthless' Victorian churches.
[2] Clarke, *op. cit.* p.80f.

ANGLO-CATHOLIC WORSHIP: AN EVANGELICAL APPRECIATION AFTER 150 YEARS

The twentieth century

In the twentieth century we see a movement away from the view that only Gothic churches are suitable for 'catholic' ceremonial. Indeed, some of the churches built for the most 'advanced' worship are in an Italianate basilican style, with some affinities with Gothic, but not at all the sort of thing the Ecclesiologists would have approved. There arose also a tendency away from putting the choir in stalls between congregation and sanctuary, so that the ceremonial could be seen uninterruptedly in its full splendour by the congregation. Some of these later 'catholic' churches have west gallery choirs and organs.

More recently, much that was distinctive in the anglo-catholic emphases has been overtaken by the liturgical movement, especially since Vatican II. Many of the tendencies in Roman Catholic worship and ordering of churches since Vatican II have left anglo-catholics 'high and dry', forced to abandon ground for which they had fought hard in the past, because their Roman mentors had abandoned it, in the ordering of churches as well as in matters cermonial.

The legacy—good or bad?

There is an immense amount that we take for granted, as a regular part of the design and furnishing of Anglican churches, which we owe directly to anglo-catholicism, and we give *some* thanks for that.

There are several things for which we are less thankful, however. We have inherited large numbers of Victorian Gothic churches, echoing pillared halls of a character inappropriate to 'renewed' worship, and often too large for the present day congregations (albeit that the kind of congregational growth of which there are signs in recent years may yet make us glad enough of the size of these buildings). The symbolism which inspired the Gothic revival no longer speaks to us today, and some of its architectural results are liabilities when stripped of their symbolism. Victorian churches tend to be cold, both physically, in that they are hard to heat at tolerable cost, but also in the sense that they lend themselves more to worship of distant and detached dignity than to warmth and friendliness. They are also hard to re-order in a way appropriate to our present ideas for worship. The eastward march of a Gothic building makes it difficult to provide a convincing centre of worship other than at the east end. Choir stalls can be moved, but what of the nearly immovable bulk of the organ? If there is a screen, that punctuates the eastward thrust, and a table can be set up in front of it, perhaps by moving some pews. But again, the Victorians tended to make things very solid, to last a thousand years, which makes them hard to remove or replace after only a hundred.[1]

So, our thanks on the anniversary to the Ecclesiologists and their successors for opening our eyes to the significance of architecture for worship. (Our thanks also for the unwitting amusement they sometimes cause us by some of their more earnest writings). But less thanks for many of the actual buildings which they have bequeathed to us.

[1] Radical re-ordering of Victorian interiors is possible—a notable recent example is St. Nicholas, Durham—but it is liable to be expensive, and when less carefully done can destroy the essential character of the building.

7. 'EVERY KNEE SHALL BOW'
by Charles Hutchins

The bowing of the head at the name of Jesus, the signing with the cross on forehead, lip, or chest, and the genuflexion before the reserved sacramental elements, are serious, helpful, and meaningful, aids to worship for many Christians. However as they appear to be empty and meaningless acts to others they have become objects of questioning or even derision to them. Candles also, to say nothing of vestments and incense, are important for many, and whilst the use of symbolism and ornate ceremonial is no longer confined to the inheritors of the Tractarian tradition[1] and there is not the debate and conflict that once there was, some ceremonial is rejected by evangelicals because the ceremonial itself is allied to unacceptable doctrine.

The introduction of 'high' cermonial into the Church of England came through the Oxford movement, and particularly in the second generation.[2] The influence of the Church of Rome upon them is acknowledged and the reaction of the general public to what was seen as the introduction of Romanism was intense. Such conflicts, ending occasionally in Privy Council or Ecclesiastical Courts[3] arose because as the Oxford movement

> 'became more parochial it acquired a heightened pragmatic interest in the externals of worship as instruments with which to disseminate tractarian teaching'.[4]

The President of the English Church Union said in 1868:

> 'nor are we merely contending for the revival among ourselves of certain ceremonies because they are practised by the rest of the Catholic Church, but we contend for our ritual for the precise reason which is urged for its suppression—because it is the means, the importance of which becomes clearer every day, which the Church has seen fit to employ to express the truth of Christ's Sacramental Presence amongst His people.'[5]

As ornate ceremonial increased and objections to wafers, lighted candles, stone Altars, and vestments, became subjects of court judgments confusion increased. In June 1867 a Royal Commission on Ritual was appointed in order to get some order and consistency. It led to the Public Worship Regulation Act of 1874. But when five clergymen were imprisoned between 1878 and 1887 as a result of the Act, the Act itself became discredited. In Bishop Bickersteth's words 'I fear that

---

[1] See N. Sagovsky *Liturgy and Symbolism* (Grove Liturgical Study 16, 1978); Kenneth Stevenson (Ed.) *Symbolism and the Liturgy 1* (Grove Liturgical Study 23, 1980); Kenneth Stevenson (Ed.) *Symbolism and the Liturgy 2* (Grove Liturgical Study 26, 1981); Trevor Lloyd *Ceremonial in Worship* (Grove Worship Series 75, 1981).

[2] A good overview can be found in David Edwards *Leaders of the Church of England 1828-1978* (Hodder and Stoughton, London, 1978) pp.54-78.

[3] See e.g. R. P. Flindall *The Church of England 1815-1948 a Documentary History* (S.P.C.K., London, 1972), pp.159-162, 'The Liddell Judgment 1857'.

[4] See L. E. Ellsworth *Charles Lowder and the Ritualist Movement* (Darton, Longman and Todd, London, 1982) p.5.

[5] W. Walsh *The Secret History of the Oxford Movement* (London 1899) p.292.

prosecutions in the court on such matters of ritual only aggravate the evils they are intended to suppress'.[1] The laity however had not always imbibed the practices beloved of the clergy. Bishop Knox, writing openly from a different conviction in 1933, recounts how he had succeeded in 1885 to a country parish of

> 'a Tractarian regime of 40 years, but did not find there ten families that could be reckoned as tinctured with High Church teaching. Spurgeon's sermons I found in many houses, Newman's not in one'.[2]

This therefore leads on to an appraisal of the various practices, what they stand for and where an evangelical with wide sympathies stands in relation to them. I start with certain things that I have experienced and respect in anglo-catholic worship, and the first is *dignity and order.*

Regrettably not all Christian worship is decent, in order, or conducted with dignity. One can (and does) attend services where nothing is well prepared, nobody knows what is likely to happen next, nor does there appear any great desire to offer the best for God. Whilst generalizations are dangerous, congregations dedicated to a ceremonial presentation of the faith in worship provide more often a framework of dignity and order within which a worshipper can sit comfortably. Manuals of how to execute the liturgy are provided[3], and worship is directed towards God and not to human back-slapping chumminess.[4]

The second element is *personal discipline* over spirituality.

In 1865 Pusey held the first Retreat in his own room at Oxford when some seventeen or eighteen clergy were present for a whole week.[5] The intention was to develop a Rule of Life and a deepening of spirituality. That it appeared such an intention was thought only obtainable by looking to Rome should not distort the evident emphasis upon the personal spiritual life and auricular confession. At St. Alphege Greenwich it became a means of enlisting an elitist group, the Church Confraternity, without which no person would be considered a member of the congregation; in Leeds scandal was caused over the introduction of confession as part of confirmation preparation.[6] Both dignity and discipline evangelicals do well to imitate. The dignity and beauty of orderly worship inbreathed by the Spirit leads those who come in from the outside to fall down and worship the Lord. Personal discipline and growth in spirituality take us further along the road of consecration and holiness, and any ceremonial helping in this without compromising biblical truth will always be taken seriously by an evangelical.

However there is another side to the coin, and to the negative we now turn.

[1] R. P. Flindall *op. cit.* p.232.
[2] E. A. Knox *The Tractarian Movement* (Putnam, London 1933) p.x, xi.
[3] See, e.g. Alcuin Club Publications—let alone the C.L.A. and A.C.S..
[4] I have attended a wedding set in the context of communion including charismatic choruses, Hail Mary, and incense. The human celebration was in no way lost, and the dignity and order of it made a highly memorable and worshipful event.
[5] See Walsh *op. cit.* pp.40-41 for fears of 'Romanizing'.
[6] S. C. Carpenter *Church and People* (S.P.C.K. 1933) p.214, and Walsh *op. cit.* p.179 and p.57.

'EVERY KNEE SHALL BOW'

We begin with gimmick and *superstition*. We may not hang a stuffed dove above the altar on Whit Sunday as an incumbent did in the 1860s in Brighton[1] but some ceremonial does still border on the superstitious. The crossing of oneself at the announcement of the Gospel may well be a legitimate aid to worship and concentration, but what can repeated crossing throughout the service, or a hasty crossing of oneself before a football match or athletic race, or even before a meal, mean? It appears superstitious. Equally the emphasis on dress or act can lead to a lack of authenticity and an undesirable emptiness and formalism.

It was alleged that prior to the Reformation it took a priest longer to discover what he should say from the various books than it did actually to say it. The possibility of empty *formalism* still lingers when emphasis on performance overshadows content. Prayers of preparation hastily muttered in the vestry or at the altar with no apparent pause or change of mood from day to day or week to week provide one example. Sometimes lay people (occasionally clerical rejects) with little spiritual life manage to land key posts in the sanctuary!

Charles Lowder at the Liverpool Congress in 1869 spoke about the centrality of the eucharist in terms very different from what has just been pictured. 'We do not gather our people together merely to hear sermons, merely to say prayers, or merely to sing hymns and psalms. That is not all. But we gather them together to kneel down in God's presence and to worship Him.'[2] True—and empty formalism can equally be found in evangelical worship, for only the Spirit gives life.

Tattiness also gives cause for concern. I caused a stir as an Area Dean during an interregnum. Being responsible for the worship in a parish which had the outward trappings of Tractarianism but no strong teaching to back it up, I objected to the candle grease, filthy vestments, and altar furnishings. To their credit things changed, but the feel of the place was still of empty formalism with little spiritual life. It was no isolated occurrence.[3] One of the great arguments for vestments outside that of doctrinal significance is colour and splendour—and that I would accept—but tattiness, whether in the state of the vestments fabric-wise or in the poor matching of copes, stoles and vestments, must be eliminated. Aesthetics are important and (to give a personal view) the over-abundance of lace creates the wrong impression. An appearance of effeminacy in the sanctuary combined with robot-type choreography detracts from the worship of God. Parishes much given to lace are often those which object to women as servers, or distributors of communion. Strange paradox!

Rome has greatly simplified recently and the Charismatic Movement has enabled many traditions to find a meeting point. When inner spiritual life matches external ceremonial, heaven comes to earth. When that is missing it would be better to abolish the external than to slip into empty formalism and superstition. The Buddhist prayer-wheels we believe are meaningless, but Christianity can and does degenerate into similar superstition, and does so tragically in ceremonial.

[1] L. E. Ellsworth *op. cit.* p.114.
[2] *Id:* p.108.
[3] Clearly that has been the case in the diocese of Southwark where the most recent Pastoral Notes issued include a Directive on this very matter.

ANGLO-CATHOLIC WORSHIP: AN EVANGELICAL APPRECIATION AFTER 150 YEARS

Finally, we ask what are the main ceremonial uses for anglo-catholics. 'The first Tractarians had been concerned purely for the renewal of doctrine: Pusey was against any obstructions of that effort by provocative trappings. But by the 1870's the High Church emphasis was on the reform of ritual'.[1]
In 1875 six points were held to be paramount: vestments, the eastward position, wafer bread, incense, altar lights, and the mixed chalice.[2]

Today westward position, for example, has usually been adopted; bread rolls are sometimes introduced; vestments have been simplified. The idea of vesting the priest in all kinds of garments with symbolic meaning, with a set pattern of order and prayers in putting them on, has been superseded by the simplified cassock-alb. The personality of the human being is now allowed to appear whereas once it was supposed to get lost in the garments. Chasubles and stoles remain, though one hears less now of their standing for a sacrificing priesthood.

There are, however, two actions which to me are sticking points, and they focus on the fundamentals which were the controversies at the Reformation. Neither was directly an issue in the sixteenth century (though both were eliminated), but the doctrines they reflect were.

Genuflexion before the consecrated elements, whether on the communion table or in the aumbry, signifies a belief in a Real Presence of Christ in (or very closely associated with) the elements. Something more than a setting apart for sacramental use is believed to have taken place and a 'localized' presence of Christ is revered.

Equally, elevation, during the eucharistic prayer, is an important action inviting adoration and arguably signifying that a sacrificial offering is taking place. In other words, these two 'sticking points' demonstrate the nub of the question.[3] A particular interpretation of consecration, which effects a unique 'Real Presence'; and particular understanding of priesthood and sacrifice which follows on from that consecration.

Evangelicals may have been over-defensive in the past.[4] But where ceremonial posture, or act, suggests misleading doctrines, an evangelical will still reject them and refuse to conform. Where however outward ceremonial does not compromise true doctrine as he sees it, he will be prepared not only to conform, but also to innovate and introduce new ceremonial.[5] He need not be defensive today.

Dare one end by asking whether current 'Catholic Renewal' implies that a previous, now 'renewed', resolve to remain traditionalist, is in view? Is 'Catholicism' integrally tied to traditional ceremonial, as a necessary expression of its particular doctrines, or has it freedom to think again and to be renewed?

---

[1] J. Whale *One Church One Lord* (S.C.M. 1979) p.121.
[2] L. E. Ellsworth *op. cit.* p.114.
[3] I recall how one fairly typical priest said to me that he would always conform in dress and ceremonial to local use wherever he was officiating, but these two actions 'I would always do wherever I was'. So what doctrines lie behind them?
[4] For a historical survey of the evangelical reaction in the early years see Peter Toon *Evangelical Theology 1833-1856* (Marshall 1979) pp.173-202.
[5] See Trevor Lloyd *Ceremonial in Worship* (Grove Worship Series 75, 1981).

8. 'HOLY CHANT AND PSALM'
by Robin Leaver

The original Tractarians and the later anglo-catholics made an immense impact on the music and hymnody of the Church of England, changing them beyond recognition. Sir Frederick Gore Ouseley, professor of music at Oxford and founder of St. Michael's, Tenbury, summarized thus at the Church Congress in Brighton, 1874:

'It is difficult in these days to realize fully the ordinary state of our country choirs a century ago. And unless we do so, we shall be unable duly to appreciate the vast improvement which has taken place in them in our days. Forty years ago this process of improvement was already going on, and the people then drew very favourable comparisons between the church music of that date and the church music of half a century sooner . . . [a] fearful chaos of hideous sounds . . . was accepted in those days as sufficiently tuneful for the service of the sanctuary . . . organs were seldom found except in large town churches. Harmoniums were then unknown. If there was any instrumental accompaniment to the psalmody, it consisted of a couple of clarionets, a bassoon, a violoncello, and sometimes a small flute. Chanting the Psalms and Canticles was a feat seldom attempted by any but cathedral and collegiate choirs . . . As for surpliced choirs in chancels, such an idea never entered people's heads for a moment in rural districts, and very rarely indeed in the towns . . . The architectural restoration of our churches also had a great influence for good on parochial choirs, for it involved the wholesale destruction of galleries and pews, and thus tended to bring the choral body into their proper position in the chancel, where . . . they could best become the choral leaders of the congregation, and . . . were duly invested in their proper robe—the surplice.'[1]

Ten years later the precentor of Chester Cathedral observed to the same assembly, then meeting in Carlisle, that 'a church without its full Choral Matins and Evensong, and in many cases without its Choral Celebration, is hard to find.'[2] And that was substantially true, for evangelicals, who had earlier dismissed the chanting of the psalms as a Romish practice to be avoided at all costs[3], were beginning to introduce it into their services,[4] even if they hesitated at that stage over surpliced choirs. Yet within a matter of a decade or two these three distinctive features of Anglican church music were almost universal, irrespective of churchmanship; surpliced choirs in the chancel, the chanting of psalms, and organs adjacent to the chancel.

But it is ironic that the first two of these features originated somewhat before the Tractarians and the third they specifically discouraged! A surpliced choir was not unknown in some town parish churches during the first quarter of the nineteenth century. For example, a surpliced

---
[1] *Church Congress* (1874) pp.96ff., cp. also p.110f.
[2] *Church Congress* (1884) p.326.
[3] See, e.g., *The Life of the Revd. William Marsh by His Daughter* (London, 1883), p.286.
[4] See J. S. Reynolds, *Canon Christopher of St. Aldate's, Oxford* (Abingdon, 1967) pp.264f and 394-397.

ANGLO-CATHOLIC WORSHIP: AN EVANGELICAL APPRECIATION AFTER 150 YEARS

choir had been introduced into Leeds parish church in 1818, although eight years later it was still being viewed as a controversial practice.[1] The congregational singing of the prose psalms to 'Anglican' chant is often stated to have been introduced as a direct result of the Oxford Movement. But since early in the century various congregations of evangelicals had been enthusiastically chanting the canticles and psalms. In the north it was centred around St. Michael le Belfrey, York, and the activities of Jonathan Gray;[2] and (mainly) in the south it was fostered by *National Psalmody* (1817), compiled by Benjamin Jacob (then organist of Rowland Hill's Surrey Chapel, London).[3] That is not to deny that later anglo-catholics spread these practices widely.

On organs the Tractarians were clear: they were essentially unnecessary. The Camden Society discouraged the use of organs at every opportunity. The *Ecclesiologist* (Vol. 3, 1843, p.5) stated that *if* an organ must be introduced it should be positioned

> 'at the west end, either of the nave or of an aisle, *and on the ground*. Then, the singers being rightly placed in the chancel, it will not drown the voices nor make them dependent on itself,'[4]

The ideal was unaccompanied singing. In 1842 E. Shuttleworth of St. Mary's, Penzance, said that there they had 'the whole service intoned admirably without instrumental accompaniment.'[5] Similarly, at St. Mark's College, Chelsea, where Thomas Helmore was vice-principal, the daily services were sung unaccompanied from 1841 to 1861.[6]

This unaccompanied singing was part of the Tractarian aim to reform the worship of the contemporary church by re-introducing ancient practices as spiritually essential. The ancient unaccompanied song of the church was Gregorian chant, and the adherents of the Oxford Movement zealously promoted its use. William Palmer had prepared the way in his *Origines Liturgicae, or Antiquities of the English Ritual* (Oxford, 1832) which had sought to demonstrate the catholic background and significance of the Prayer Book. Thus it was legitimate and desirable to employ the chant associated with ancient uses for the Prayer Book orders. These nineteenth century reformers regarded themselves as Prayer Book loyalists,[7] and they were particularly gratified to discover John Marbeck's *Book of Common Prayer Noted* (1550), in which Prayer Book services are set to a simplified form of

---

[1] See B. Rainbow, *The Choral Revival in the Anglican Church (1839-1872)*, (London, 1970) pp.307ff.

[2] See N. Temperley, *Jonathan Gray and Church Music in York 1770-1840*, (York, 1977), pp.17ff. The parish has pioneered again in recent years, we hear.

[3] Four-part chants are included for most of the Prayer Book Canticles (but not the Venite), as well as four-part settings of the Responses to the Decalogue and Sanctus in the Communion Service.

[4] John Mason Neale, in a Camden Society tract of the same year, *Church Enlargement and Church Arrangement* (quoted at length in Rainbow, *op. cit.*, pp.319-321) made the same point. However, John Jebb, in *The Choral Service of the United Church of England and Ireland* (London, 1843) p.153, was commending chancel organs as the right position 'according to ancient usage'.

[5] See N. Temperley, *The Music of the English Parish Church* (Cambridge, 1979) p.253.

[6] An organ was introduced into the college chapel in 1861; see Rainbow, *op. cit.* p.50.

[7] *The Parish Choir*, Vol. 1, No. 1 (Feb., 1846) p.2.

Gregorian chant.[1] Although some acknowledged Marbeck's protestantism[2], most simply assumed that his aim was to preserve traditional Gregorian chant for English use.[3] During the years 1843-45 significant editions were issued, to encourage the use of plainchant settings of the Prayer Book services.[4] All were simple, unaccompanied, and monodic. But in 1846 *The Parish Choir* gave Marbeck's chants for Morning and Evening Prayer, as well as for communion (adapted from 1549 for 1662), with simple four-part accompaniment—a move to make the somewhat austere music more palatable.

Marbeck's book was followed by Helmore's *The Psalter Noted* (1849), which is clearly derived from Marbeck's title.[5] In 1851 Helmore and Neale produced *The Hymnal Noted*[6], an office hymn book of translated Latin hymns and plainsong tunes.[7] This trilogy was thought of as providing all the necessary music for the Prayer Book. Although hymns like *O come, O come, Emmanuel, Christ is made the sure foundation,* and *All glory, laud and honour* have come into use via *The Hymnal Noted,* and Marbeck's setting, has become widely used, yet the hopes of the early Tractarians have never been realized as a whole.

The problem was that such unaccompanied music sounded austere and foreign to the ordinary English ear. It needed harmony—but then organs and trained choirs were thought of as necessities—and they followed thick and fast. In that 1874 address Ouseley specifically attributed the improvements in church music to the widespread introduction of organs and harmoniums.[8] The anglo-catholics' model was the cathedral music tradition now adapted for parish use.[9] They were astonishingly successful in establishing what has become known as the 'Anglican' tradition of church music. Even though plainchant was never far away, the tendency was towards rich and elaborate music, especially at celebrations of high mass. In 1881 masses by Mozart, Schubert and Cherubini could be heard, often complete with orchestral accompaniment, in many churches.[10] Yet at the same time as surpliced choirs rendered such highly artistic music, anglo-catholic congregations were singing incredibly subjective and sentimental hymns.

---

[1] For the background to this rediscovery see R. A. Leaver, *The Work of John Marbeck* (Courtenay Library of Reformation Classics 9), (Appleford, 1978), pp.9-21.

[2] See *The Parish Choir,* Vol. 1, No. 2 (March, 1846) p.15.

[3] Marbeck did simplify traditional chants but also composed new ones. For the details see R. A. Leaver, *Marbeck's Book of Common Prayer Noted (1550)* (Courtenay Facsimile 3) (Appleford, 1982) pp.56-76; see also Leaver, *op. cit., p.14f.*

[4] See Leaver, *The Work of John Marbeck,* p.13f.

[5] *Canticles Noted* followed in 1850. Later the two publications were combined, with a Marbeck appendix, to form *The Manual of Plainsong,* (still in print).

[6] See P. Westermeyer, 'The Hymnal Noted: Theological and Musical Intersections,' *Church Music 73.2* (1973) pp.1-9.

[7] Newman had pointed the way with his translations of Latin Breviary hymns, issued with Tract 75 *On the Roman Breviary* (1836), and his collection *Hymni Ecclesiae,* 1838. Later Helmore was arguing for a common hymnal, authorized by Convocation, which would, like *The Hymnal Noted,* consist principally of the ancient Latin office hymns in English dress; (see *Church Congress* (1879), p.345).

[8] *op. cit.,* p.97.

[9] Ouseley in 1872 refused to distinguish any longer cathedral from parochial music.

[10] F. J. Crowest, *Phases of Musical England* (London, 1881) p.73f. These followed Roman usage; see M. Hurd *Vincent Novello and Company* (London, 1981).

ANGLO-CATHOLIC WORSHIP: AN EVANGELICAL APPRECIATION AFTER 150 YEARS

This is characteristic of anglo-catholicism, which has either pursued its high ideals at the expense of popularity, or sought popularity by sacrificing its ideals. For example, *Hymns Ancient and Modern* was first issued in 1861 as a self-consciously Tractarian collection.[1] However, in order to broaden its appeal a supplement was added in 1868 containing a wider selection.[2] The process of expansion continued until '*A. & M.*' became the broad church hymnal used in many differing parishes. Then attempts were made to restore the objective stance in anglo-catholic congregational worship. In 1904 a new edition of *Hymns Ancient and Modern* was prepared, largely under the guidance of W. H. Frere, who was critical of popular anglo-catholicism which rendered the congregation largely mute.[3] The same year saw G. R. Woodward's *Songs of Syon,* but it was far too antiquarian in its approach. In 1906 *The English Hymnal* appeared under the expert musical editorship of Ralph Vaughan Williams, and Percy Dearmer.[4] Dearmer succeeded where Frere and Woodward failed, largely because of his judicious blend of the ancient office hymns in translation with a fine selection of distinctive English hymnody. It has influenced all hymn books since, though it never matched *A. & M.* for popularity.

In retrospect we must be grateful to the Tractarians and their successors for teaching us that music has an important place in liturgical worship, even though we regret the stylized pattern of chancel organs and choirs which effectively silenced congregations for so long. Time and again it has been argued that there are good *musical* reasons for east-end music.[5] But the reasons are essentially theological. There are, in fact, good acoustic reasons for having the organ and choir in a west gallery, as before Tractarian restorations. Church music in those days left much to be desired, but what was needed was reform, and not wholesale destruction and rebuilding, as enlightened anglo-catholics at the turn of the century saw only too clearly.[6] But the theological emphasis has shifted and there is now a greater stress on the whole people of God at worship. In consequence choirs are coming out of chancels, organs are being placed elsewhere and various accompanying instruments are being used. Our church music is becoming more varied. But that it is now on the liturgical agenda is due in no small measure to the Tractarians and their successors.

[1] W. K. Lowther Clarke, *A Hundred Years of Hymns and Ancient and Modern* (London, 1960) p.31, called it 'a Tractarian Manifesto'. Curiously, there were then only five communion hymns—the days of the sung eucharist were yet to come.

[2] The 113 hymns included six more for communion, and three for processions.

[3] W. H. Frere, *The Principles of Religious Ceremonial* (London, 1928²) p.35f.

[4] 'Probably the silencing of all the organs for a period of ten years would make our churches into nests of singing birds. For organs have become like alcohol,' (*The Art of Public Worship* (London, 1920) p.89.)

[5] See, e.g. S. H. Nicholson, *Quires and Places Where They Sing* (London, 1932) p.188.

[6] 'The west gallery is the proper place for the organ, and to the west gallery let it be restored, even if the choir must be left at the east end . . . we never did a worse day's work than when we dis-established the old village orchestra . . .' H. C. Shuttleworth, *The Place of Music in Public Worship* (London, 1892) p.57; 'But shall we ever recover church music until we have a music-gallery, and . . . village fellowship until we have a village band?' (Dearmer, *op. cit.,* p.89).